Every Day w

Jesu

MAY/JUN 2022

C000139101

WAVERLEY ABBEY
RESOURCES

MIX
Paper from
responsible sources
FSC® C021017
www.fsc.org

James 5:13–16

'Is anyone among you in trouble? Let them pray. Is anyone happy? Let them sing songs of praise. Is anyone among you ill? Let them call the elders of the church to pray over them and anoint them with oil in the name of the Lord.' (vv13–14)

Prayer is foundational in learning to live every day with Jesus successfully. Many of us find that prayer is elusive; simple to grasp the principles involved, yet difficult to execute satisfactorily. Many express concern that they do not pray enough, where a precise measure for 'enough' is impossible to quantify. Scripture presents countless examples of calls to prayer. The book of Psalms, often referred to as the songbook of the Bible, is essentially a prayer book. Over this next month we shall explore the foundations for prayer throughout the Bible, as well as offer some practical guidelines and support as we each seek to nurture our personal prayer life. Whilst 'trouble' is a significant provocation for prayer – and the *Church Times* reported a survey's findings, published by Tearfund, that one in twenty adults started praying during lockdown, despite not praying before* – trouble is not the *primary* reason to pray. Prayer deepens our friendship, understanding and appreciation for God. Much like conversation strengthens relationships, so prayer is to take personal time with God. Whilst it involves thanksgiving, confession, making requests and quiet contemplation, not one of these elements constitutes prayer on its own. Prayer is something that takes a lifetime to learn, and deepens only as we invest time to discover how we may personally encounter God. Prayer is not a duty to compete or a ritual to perform; it's a school of learning intimacy with our heavenly Father. It is the space into which we confidently carry our personal business with God.

SCRIPTURE TO CONSIDER: Ps. 139:1–12; Jer. 29:11–14; Rom. 8:22–27; Rev. 3:14–22.

AN ACTION TO TAKE: Honestly consider the condition of your prayer life? Is there room for development?

A PRAYER TO MAKE: 'Lord, I am excited to join You in Your school of prayer. Amen.'

* edwj.org/mj22-1may [accessed 13/02/2022]

Mark 1:32–35
'Very early in the morning, while it was still dark, Jesus got up, left the house and went off to a solitary place, where he prayed.' (v35)

L iving every day with Jesus is to discover how to grow as a disciple by considering all Jesus said and did. Here, at the start of Mark's Gospel, we see Jesus getting up 'very early' to pray. There is nothing sacred about first light, but I, like many, find this the best time for personal prayer. There are very few distractions, and the symbolism of the dawn is a stimulus for prayer. What's most important is to find our own 'solitary place' in life's busyness in which to encounter God. Jesus was disturbed by His disciples, and our days present constant interruptions and demands that risk robbing us of quality time with God. There are always arrow prayers when busy, but a relationship must suffer when continually interrupted by the incessant stream of daily demands. Activity displaces presence even as intimacy deteriorates.

It's important to learn how to establish a prayer life and create time alone with God. We're challenged by confusion, not knowing where to begin, whilst also suffering from doubts and fears. School exists to teach us how to navigate life. In same way, this solitary place becomes our schoolroom, essential for learning faithfulness in living and serving God in a secular society. We also need fellowship, but not in exchange for our personal, intimate relationship with God. We cannot afford to rely on being carried on the worship of God's people alone. Jesus ensured He got this balance absolutely right; without it He would have struggled to fulfil His ministry on earth.

SCRIPTURE TO CONSIDER: Gen. 32:24–32; Jer. 9:1–6; Mark 6:30–34; Luke 5:12–16.

AN ACTION TO TAKE: How do you find the thought of a solitary prayer space? Will you organise to take time alone with God and free from distraction every day?

A PRAYER TO MAKE: 'Lord, help me to establish a time and space where You and I can meet alone every day. Amen.'

Write to micha@edwj.org and I'll write back personally and in confidence as soon as I can.

Psalm 1:1–3

'but whose delight is in the law of the LORD, and who meditates on his law day and night. That person is like a tree planted by streams of water, which yields its fruit in season'(vv2–3a)

Today we're fascinated by output. We've learnt to measure outcomes, but not to value content and process. Prayer is the process of seeking God with a twofold objective; to deepen our appreciation and understanding of God primarily, and consequently to begin to think and live by God's desire and not our instinctive preferences. Prayer, whilst generally affirmed by all Christians, often finds little place in our Christian activities. We are better seeing it as a lifestyle than an action we execute. Scripture suggests it forms part of every waking and sleeping hour. We learn to dwell in God's presence continually, something Paul highlights in his encouragement that we are to 'pray continually' (1 Thess. 5:17).

In an age increasingly consumed with ideas of wellbeing, how remarkable that prayer is good for our physical, mental and emotional health.* Centred on God, we can expect to live a virtuous life, and we do not wither when the burdens of life threaten to overwhelm us. So many of the wellbeing techniques promoted for our overall health are themselves the practices that have marked the lives of God's followers for centuries. I am myself so grateful to the sayings of the Desert Mothers and Fathers, as well as the extensive writings of the Church Fathers. Following the path of a contemplative has both radically reduced my anxiety and also renewed my engagement with life at every level. My one desire, to sink my roots ever deeper into the refreshing resource of God's love (Jer. 17:7–8).

SCRIPTURE TO CONSIDER: Ps. 139:13–18; Prov. 12:15–28; John 15:1–17; Eph. 1:15–23.

AN ACTION TO TAKE: Does prayer feature on your wellbeing schedule? Learning to take time with God and become aware of God's presence throughout the day is good for us.

A PRAYER TO MAKE: Lord, help me to become aware of Your presence morning, noon and night by God's grace. Amen.'

* edwj.org/mj22-3may [accessed 13/02/2022]

E-Learning Short Courses

Feed your mind in your own time and at a pace that suits you best. Ideal for individuals, small groups and congregations.

 Insight Courses

 Paraclesis:
A series on pastoral care

 The Prayers of Jesus

 Eat, Pray, Share

These and other courses are all available for you online at a price of £25 each.

To find out more and to buy a course, visit

wvly.org/online-courses

Our Father

Matthew 6:5–15

'But when you pray, go into your room, close the door and pray to your Father, who is unseen. Then your Father, who sees what is done in secret, will reward you.' (v6)

J esus taught His disciples one prayer, the foundation and framework for all prayer. Matthew encourages us to separate ourselves and, in solitude, use this prayer. Today, whilst included in most mainstream liturgies, it's less frequently used in independent congregations. Perhaps there's room to rethink its use if absent, since these are the words Jesus actually spoke. It covers both our worship as well as expressing our needs. Short and to the point, it effectively provides all that we need to include in prayer; encouraging when circumstances rob us of the energy to pray more extensively.

The Lord's Prayer provides us with a simple, yet practical framework on which we can build the whole pattern of our prayers, from praise to provision. I use it frequently throughout my day. It is amongst the few prayers I make on opening my eyes each morning before getting out of bed. I refuse to start my day ahead of prayer, for it is in prayer that I am reminded of my devotion to God and of my responsibility to put His interests first in my daily thoughts and actions. I love its simplicity and clarity, reminding me that prayers are not theological compendiums, but a simple outpouring of my heart to God. Simplicity is key to effective prayer, for it clarifies what we are expressing to God, without compromise or double mindedness. Sometimes I pause in recognition of the promise I am making through my prayer – a pause to consider if my commitment can really support my words.

SCRIPTURE TO CONSIDER: Ps. 24:1–6; 96:4–13; Matt. 6:25–34; Rom. 14:12–23.

AN ACTION TO TAKE: The best response is to decide if you might say the Lord's Prayer daily or not. Might it prove a useful starting point to your day? Your decision!

A PRAYER TO MAKE: 'Lord, may Your kingdom come and Your will be done on earth as it is in heaven. Amen.'

Luke 11:1–8

'I tell you, even though he will not get up and give you the bread because of friendship, yet because of your shameless audacity he will surely get up and give you as much as you need.' (v8)

It's important to note in Luke's account that the Lord's Prayer emerges from the disciples' observation of how Jesus chose to live. Whilst it can be challenging to make time to pray once our day has gathered momentum, it remains important that we do pray. It is why my preference is to pray before my day begins. This means setting my alarm to allow for a good time for prayer and contemplation before my routine kicks in. I have my place of solitude where I sit away from distractions. This is a place that I use consistently for prayer and for nothing else but reading. Jesus took Himself away, alone and at a time when He wouldn't be interrupted.

All prayer is best begun with considering God, and here we acknowledge God's name, kingdom and will. God's will is His kingdom, which is why it is not found in some manuscripts. So we start by considering God, not ourselves. But then we are to appeal to God for our provision, pardon and protection, the basics that ensure we can continue to love and serve God. Indeed, the Lord's Prayer illustrates how simple the Christian life is meant to be. Jesus summarised the Law as loving God and neighbour, and we do this through honouring God's name whilst submitting to His will. It is then that we are encouraged by God's goodness expressed throughout life even as circumstances blur our vision or seek to strike fear within our hearts.

SCRIPTURE TO CONSIDER: Deut. 6:4–12; Zeph. 3:14–20; Mark 12:28–34; John 3:16–21.

AN ACTION TO TAKE: It's a challenge to measure our life against God's simple plan. Is simplicity something that attracts us? If not, why?

A PRAYER TO MAKE: 'Lord, help me to build my life upon Your two priorities; loving God and loving neighbour. Amen.'

Our Prayers

1 Timothy 2:1–8

'I urge, then, first of all, that petitions, prayers, intercession and thanksgiving be made for all people – for kings and all those in authority, that we may live peaceful and quiet lives in all godliness and holiness.' (vv1–2)

The Lord's Prayer is in the first person plural (*Our* Father, forgive *us*, lead *us*, etc). Whilst we know God personally, we always pray as members of God's global community, the Church. Our personal church preference is itself just one small expression of the invisible Church, known to God alone and in contrast to the visible, or institutional constructs of human invention, both large and small. The whole Church prays; my voice is just one amongst Christ's choir, hymning His name, and prayerfully encircling the globe continuously.

Timothy identifies four elements to help us pray. Petitions are a formal, written request made to an official person, in this case God Himself. They are best expressed in simple, clear terms. Don't worry about how you frame your petitions, just make them known to God. Too many words and we become like babbling pagans (Matt. 6:7). Intercession, by contrast, is to empathise and stand before God on behalf of the person or cause we're presenting. It's an intervention for their benefit. Prayers are personalised expressions of our worship, whilst thanksgiving expresses gratitude. So, in answer to the question, 'Am I praying enough?' that often nags at our conscience, the Lord's Prayer plus a petition, an intercession for a situation like a personal or national crisis, a remembrance of God's grace and glory, and time taken to say thank you makes up a wonderful prayer time. God always looks at our heart and not the clock! Let us learn to 'waste' more time with God.

SCRIPTURE TO CONSIDER: 1 Sam. 1:21–28; Jer. 42:1–12; Acts 12:1–19; Phil. 4:4–9.

AN ACTION TO TAKE: Why not note down Timothy's simple template from Scripture and adopt it every day to guide your prayer?

A PRAYER TO MAKE: 'Lord, thank You that You look on my heart and that I can make my simple requests known to You. Amen.'

Hebrews 7:22–28

'but because Jesus lives for ever, he has a permanent priesthood. Therefore he is able to save completely those who come to God through him, because he always lives to intercede for them.' (vv24–25)

I n Scripture we learn that God chose the tribe of Levi to act as priests for the Israelites. They ministered before the Lord (1 Chron. 16:4) and were sustained by the offerings brought to fulfil the sacrificial system at the heart of Israelite worship (Leviticus 1–10). Jesus Himself came to earth and ministered as directed by God. He became the ultimate sacrifice, a declaration of love from God for His creation. Consequently, the blood sacrifice system ended on Calvary. Now, with the relationship between God and humanity restored through Jesus' sacrifice, we are invited to bring daily offerings of prayer to God directly. Prayer is the heart of daily worship once we acknowledge our complete dependence on God.

Yet, the wonder is that God actually invites us into His throne room to present our prayers (Heb. 4:16). Here, the resurrected and ascended Jesus intercedes continuously on our behalf before God (Rom. 8:34). Whenever we pray, we are also consistently and constantly held in Jesus' prayer. This is an encouraging reflection whenever we feel isolated, perhaps even abandoned, reminding us that we worship a God who can empathise with us for He has been tempted in every way as us (Heb. 4:15). In a similar fashion we too can intercede, holding others with their needs before God in His throne room, from where the King delivers His decisions with all the authority of His office. So we do not pray alone, but in concert with Jesus.

SCRIPTURE TO CONSIDER: Gen. 14:11–24; Ps. 110; Rom. 8:31–39; Heb. 4:14–5:10.

AN ACTION TO TAKE: When you pray, remember you're invited into God's throne room, to share your petitions, prayers, intercessions and thanksgivings. What is your response?

A PRAYER TO MAKE: 'Lord, I give You thanks that I am invited to come to the seat of Your authority and power with my prayers, and that Jesus prays with me. Amen.'

Numbers 28:1–10
'The LORD said to Moses, "Give this command to the Israelites and say to them: 'Make sure that you present to me at the appointed time my food offerings, as an aroma pleasing to me.'"' (vv1–2)

A framework for prayer is always useful, but only of value if we find a way to use it. God teaches Moses a rhythm; the sacrifice of prayer twice a day, morning and at twilight. It's a very useful, and simple, twice-daily routine to bring our petitions, prayers, intercessions and thanksgiving to God. It demands discipline, best served by setting aside specific times. These will occasionally be missed due to life's demands, but this is not to distress us. It still provides a useful framework and ensures we shall actually pray regularly.

Once a week we're invited to enjoy a Sabbath, a day off from our normal work. Traditionally a Sunday, yet in a world where commerce never stops we may find our Sabbath on a different day. Most churches still meet on Sunday, so we may miss out on what is an excellent congregational opportunity to pray. Hence we must explore how we can respond with an additional time with God on *our* Sabbath. Online offers us more opportunity today, but Sabbath is rest within the context of reflecting together with others on the grace we enjoy through Jesus. The coronavirus pandemic, whilst dramatically interrupting our customary way of living, may have created an opportunity to rethink many of our assumptions about congregational life. So this is a season through which the Church can again explore what Sabbath worship looks like in an uncertain world, where increasing numbers find Sunday doesn't offer them an opportunity to rest as God teaches.

SCRIPTURE TO CONSIDER: Ps. 4:4–8; 55:1–19; Mark 2:23–28; Col. 2:16–23.

AN ACTION TO TAKE: Would it prove helpful to decide on a daily prayer rhythm for your life?

A PRAYER TO MAKE: 'Lord, I'm grateful that I can pray to You morning and evening and celebrate Your grace on my Sabbath rest day. Amen.'

Genesis 18:16–33
'Then Abraham approached him and said: "Will you sweep away the righteous with the wicked? What if there are fifty righteous people in the city? Will you really sweep it away and not spare the place for the sake of the fifty righteous people in it?"'(vv23–24)

We have identified intercession as distinct from petition as it seeks to speak on behalf of some external need. Here Abraham intercedes for the righteous, those who serve God with integrity, in Sodom. Witness God's patience as Abraham politely, but persistently, negotiates on behalf of the lives of the righteous. Our learning is that God is indeed gracious and patient with our intercessions, and we are always learners. So often we don't know how to pray for someone, yet God invites us to pray as we can, not as we can't. There are no barriers between us and God. There are no formal rules governing how we are to carry our concerns to Him. Of course, the story reveals that Sodom is destroyed, although Lot, Abraham's relative, is saved. There were self-evidently not even ten righteous people in Sodom, and Abraham's intercession was unable to save the city. Our intercession is always in heartfelt response to situations and people, seeking to represent their real needs to God. We do not hold the keys to altering God's mind and actions, yet we can know that our intercessions are heard; we must equally accept that God not only hears but takes them into consideration. However, God's purpose, and action, lies far beyond our understanding. Intercession enables us to express our kindness and concern, yet the outcome is always something we must entrust to God. Faith is always expressed through our ultimate trust in God, and never from the measurable fruit of our intercession alone.

SCRIPTURE TO CONSIDER: 2 Chron. 7:11–16; 1 Kings 13:1–10; 2 Cor. 5:1–10; Eph. 6:18–24.

AN ACTION TO TAKE: Intercession can seem confusing, but through it we bring the needs of others to God in prayer. Who are you holding before God in prayer?

A PRAYER TO MAKE: 'Lord, I carry the concerns of friends and family, neighbour and friend, and by faith present them to You in my intercessions. Amen.'

Genesis 24:1–9

'"If the woman is unwilling to come back with you, then you will be released from this oath of mine. Only do not take my son back there." So the servant put his hand under the thigh of his master Abraham and swore an oath to him concerning this matter.' (vv8–9)

Prayer is never to force God's hand. God established free will at the creation. Adam and Eve enjoyed choice in exercising obedience to God's word. This free will has accompanied humanity from that point forward. However, Abraham had himself been guided by the intervention of an angel at the moment he was about to sacrifice his son, Isaac (Gen. 22:10–12). That angel is the Word of God, and now Abraham instructs his servant, placing complete confidence in God's word as the means by which his prayer can be fulfilled. The servant trusts Abraham's faith, and through his prayer witnesses God's word in action in response to Abraham's prayer (Gen. 24:12–13).

It's important to note that Abraham does not demand his will is fulfilled (Gen 24:8). His servant is only obliged to honour Abraham's preference expressed through prayer. This is important for we can become tongue tied and stagnate, worrying about the prayers we have made that apparently remain unanswered. Prayer is always to pursue God's Word in the context into which we pray. The outworking of such well-intentioned prayer is for the Word of God to be seen within human affairs. Our responsibility is obedience, to give expression to what we sense is the appropriate content of our prayer. We cannot exercise control over the outcome; this is at God's discretion alone. We may only ever pray by faith and trust in God's grace in action, the fruit of which may well be hidden from our sight.

SCRIPTURE TO CONSIDER: Gen. 24:34–54; Prov. 3:1–8; John 20:24–29; Heb. 11:1–6.

AN ACTION TO TAKE: How free are you with God in your prayers? Is yours the prayer of faith?

A PRAYER TO MAKE: 'Lord, I bring my preferences to You in prayer and trust their outworking through Your grace. Amen.'

John 16:12–15
'He will glorify me because it is from me that he will receive what he will make known to you.'(v14)

We can find ourselves praying because of circumstance. I well remember when Katey (my first wife) and I were told we couldn't have children; we turned to God in urgent prayer. We had a need and we figured God would fix it. Our new-found fervency in prayer, driven by our own selfish need, was surprised to find that God fondly welcomed us. Thrilled to have us praying so regularly, and taking us at our word that we wanted to surrender to Him, He invited us to address a host of issues, yet not one was our need for children. We discovered that God works in prayer to nurture our understanding of Himself, which in turn schools us in holy obedience. We two disobedient disciples reacted before finding the humility to yield to God's way.

In prayer, we hear God and discover both His purpose and will. Only as we do can our prayers come into alignment with His plan, not for our lives, but for the world we are called to serve. God is the antidote to selfishness since His actions are always in the interests of others. As we learn to live God's way, we discover how to pray for God's will and kingdom. And where we are unable to utter prayer within us, the Spirit Himself speaks to all God is in reality revealing, even whilst it remains hidden to our conscious understanding. The wonder in it all is that God wants to reveal everything about Himself to us (v15).

SCRIPTURE TO CONSIDER: Ps. 40:4–8; Lam. 2:15–19; Luke 12:1–12; Rom. 8:9–17.

AN ACTION TO TAKE: Are there areas into which you'd prefer God not to speak? Why is that?

A PRAYER TO MAKE: 'Lord, open my ears that I might hear Your voice clearly and order my life in ways that You direct. Amen.'

Write to micha@edwj.org and I'll write back personally and in confidence as soon as I can.

Leviticus 2:1–3
**'When anyone brings a grain offering to the LORD,
their offering is to be of the finest flour. They are
to pour olive oil on it, put incense on it' (v1)**

Prayer is an offering we bring in demonstration of our confidence in God. It's like a present, and we want the gift to reflect our perception of the recipient as well as to be valued by them. So our prayer is to originate from a pure heart. Whilst Old Testament (OT) offerings may seem antiquated and no longer relevant, the basis on which they were established remains true today. God calls on us to bring the very best of ourselves before Him and to ensure that our prayer is pure and true. Too often we can stumble into God's presence from a sense of duty or for self-centred, even self-indulgent reasons. Then our sacrifice of prayer is tainted and unacceptable to the Lord.

We all have needs and God is aware of these. Many are common to everyone, such as the need for a job, a home and food. However, God invites us to pray always with the needs of others in view. As we noted, the Lord's Prayer is in the plural; it's inclusive of everyone. Also our forgiveness is directly related to the forgiveness we extend to others. Christianity serves the world by following Jesus' example and putting others first, and we can most easily do this through our prayers. Anyone we pass and circumstances we observe are all available to be presented in prayer to God. One reason we are able to pray without ceasing (1 Thess. 5:17).

SCRIPTURE TO CONSIDER: Gen. 4:1–12; Isa. 66:18–24; 1 John 2:18–29; Jude 1:17–25.

AN ACTION TO TAKE: Consider if your offering of prayer is pure. How might you practise Paul's instruction to pray without ceasing?

A PRAYER TO MAKE: 'Lord, may my eyes and ears be always open to note everything that I can bring as an offering of prayer to You every day. Amen.'

Write to micha@edwj.org and I'll write back personally and in confidence as soon as I can.

1 Samuel 1:9–17
'As she kept on praying to the LORD, Eli observed her mouth. Hannah was praying in her heart, and her lips were moving but her voice was not heard. Eli thought she was drunk and said to her, "How long are you going to stay drunk? Put away your wine."' (vv12–14)

I like to mouth my prayers silently and so prevent my mind from wandering and pursuing its own many thought trails. I don't focus on each phrase's content, but remain focused on the purpose of my prayer. The mind is a challenge for each of us when praying, and we can emerge from our personal time with God with no remembrance of our actual prayers. Other factors can equally distract us from our intention to pray. Emotional disturbances easily overwhelm us, as we're engaged in processing feelings and the thought patterns they give birth to. Eli assumes that Hannah is drunk; how easily we too can judge others inappropriately. We're not to focus on another's approach to God, but give our full attention to our own. 'Keep your eyes on the road' as we navigate our own walk of faith.

Another issue that impedes our prayer is when we face pain, physical and psychological. All of our energy is needed to manage the intrusive distress the pain produces. Here it's good to have some familiar prayers which we can mouth without a second thought (eg the Lord's Prayer and Psalm 23). It's one reason I've a set form of prayer each morning, prayers I can draw on without a second thought. It is also good to remember that those who are struggling need my prayers, whether I know them or not. Prayer offers the encouragement of knowing that, whilst there are no simple answers, we are also sustained in the prayers of friend and stranger alike.

SCRIPTURE TO CONSIDER: Eccles. 9:11–18; Ps. 19:7–14; Matt. 15:7–20; Eph. 4:20–32.

AN ACTION TO TAKE: Struggling to find ways to pray without ceasing? Try praying for every person you pass in the street or as you drive along. A simple blessing will do.

A PRAYER TO MAKE: 'Lord, bless, keep and be gracious to this person and may they find true peace. Amen.'

1 Samuel 2:1–3

'Do not keep talking so proudly or let your mouth speak such arrogance, for the LORD is a God who knows, and by him deeds are weighed.' (v3)

Hannah returns to place her son, the fruit of her prayer, into Eli's care for training in God's service. Her painful petitions gave rise to his birth. It is amazing how the process of prayer can alter our whole perspective of ourselves, our world and our circumstances. This is a measure of God's engagement with us as we pray. The Spirit is at work, and our preconceptions are changed throughout our prayer life. The woman who we first meet in a wretched state is now confidently proclaiming God's name; her view of life is altogether different. Prayer is one space in which God's Spirit is always at work deep within us. This is the true work of transformation, a long word meaning 'to change form'. In other words, as I pray I'm changing.

Too often prayer is seen as something I do for God, a response, a pouring out of myself. Yet, usually unseen, there is also an in-pouring of God's grace into my being as part of the discipleship-development programme ordered by the same Holy Spirit. Hannah's understanding and approach has changed completely. It's not that she fell pregnant and had a child, but she understands something of God's purpose for her child of promise, which she may well have missed had she simply fallen pregnant as expected. Now she could release this longed-for child to serve God. This is a reminder that prayer is always a deepening of our understanding of, and ultimately deeper surrender to, God's purpose.

SCRIPTURE TO CONSIDER: Deut. 12:8–11; Isa. 12; Luke 1:46–56; Phil. 3:1–14.

AN ACTION TO TAKE: What can we do when we struggle with how to pray or feel our prayer lives are lacking? Pick up a copy of *Seven Ways to Pray* by Amy Boucher Pye: edwj.org/mj22-14may

A PRAYER TO MAKE: 'Lord, change me by Your Spirit within Your school of prayer. Amen.'

John 17:1–5
'I have brought you glory on earth by finishing the work you gave me to do. And now, Father, glorify me in your presence with the glory I had with you before the world began.' (vv4–5)

J esus tells His disciples that life presents problems (John 16:33), and then immediately turns to prayer. Our response to life's disappointments and troubles is to start praying. Our heart rate may be pumping with anxiety, and our mind filled with catastrophic thoughts, but we are best to pray at such times. This means looking towards heaven as the source of our hope and true future. Jesus' divinity is still veiled by His humanity yet, knowing His destiny, He asks God to glorify Him, and in doing so to demonstrate the authority of the Trinity. Even as He faces the challenge of Calvary, Jesus prays outward; first for His immediate disciples, then for all those who will subsequently find hope in Christ.

Life too easily directs our attention to spotlight our own troubles. There may be nothing we can do to ease our load, and narrowing our focus to our problem alone will only increase its weight on our shoulders. We are often diminished as a consequence. Prayer is the vehicle which can lift first our eyes, then our hearts, as we gaze into the face of the risen Jesus (no stranger to pain), who carries our suffering whilst easing our burden. This is no quick fix or magic mantra. It is the carefully crafted path along which we're invited to walk to maintain faith before what appear impossible obstacles. Prayer is indeed a school, with difficult lessons, yet is always the path to deepening faith and friendship with God.

SCRIPTURE TO CONSIDER: Matt. 11:25–30; Luke 22:24–38; Acts 7:54–60; Heb. 9:15–28.

AN ACTION TO TAKE: Are you enrolled in God's school of prayer? What lessons do you find most difficult?

A PRAYER TO MAKE: 'Lord, may my prayers be the crumbs with which You create a meal to nurture and nourish my faith every day. Amen.'

Acts 10:1–8

'Cornelius stared at him in fear. "What is it, Lord?" he asked. The angel answered, "Your prayers and gifts to the poor have come up as a memorial offering before God."' (v4)

I've frequently been asked by those who are not disciples if they can pray to God. Here we have a wonderful story for all our encouragement. A godly Gentile is commended by God's messenger for his prayer and his generosity. God's intention is that all should have the opportunity to receive the good news message of salvation (John 3:16). Often the journey starts with a prayer. I certainly prayed years before I was a Christian. Part as an insurance policy, and in part through superstition – just in case. No doubt these prayers, despite my life being far from devout, provided the crumbs with which the Spirit started His work of drawing me into friendship with God. God will work with whatever threads we offer and begin to weave our salvation story.

It is also interesting to note that Cornelius did not come to God, but God came to him; first with an angelic visit and then one from the apostle Peter. Peter is the rock upon which Jesus declared the Church would be built. Here the Church is missional, ie open to be sent rather than static, and seeking ways to draw the seekers into its orbit. Just as Jesus came in search of us, sent by His Father, so we are to go out to those who at present have no commitment to God's ways and be prepared to answer their questions and offer our prayer. The Church must always be in search of those who have lost their way.

SCRIPTURE TO CONSIDER: Ps. 25:1–7; 66:8–20; Luke 15:1–10; Acts 2:38–47.

AN ACTION TO TAKE: Uncertain if God will hear your prayer? Offer it to God in sincerity and call out for His grace.

A PRAYER TO MAKE: 'Lord, 'turn to me and be gracious to me, for I am lonely and afflicted'. Amen.' (Ps. 25:16)

Write to micha@edwj.org and I'll write back personally and in confidence as soon as I can.

1 Kings 19:9–13
'After the earthquake came a fire, but the LORD was not in the fire. And after the fire came a gentle whisper. When Elijah heard it, he pulled his cloak over his face and went out and stood at the mouth of the cave.' (vv12–13)

Prayer offers us a sacred space in which God can work. Sacred means a place and time we set aside to be alone with God. In other words, it's a 'Godspace' – where we deliberately step aside from the normal distractions of life. Prayer, self-evidently, is continuous when we choose to practise it as Paul encourages (1 Thess. 5:17), but there can be set times of more focused prayer. Here God meets with us, just as we are choosing to meet with Him. It is the space in which God nurtures our life in Him so that we grow towards maturity in Christ, in both thought and action (Eph. 4:15).

Like Elijah, we will experience the wind of disturbance stirring our life and alerting us to what thwarts God. It can blow dust into our eyes, or disperse the fog that's grounded us. Then there's the earthquake threatening destruction to all those we rely on and hold dear. God may send fire to consume everything ungodly in our life. Through prayer we offer our lives up for God's inspection. It is a place in which God speaks to us, not merely where we talk with God. Finally, we may encounter the gentle whisper, the presence of God with us – with the assurance that God is our fullness of life wherever we find ourselves. Jesus encourages us to find a personal space where He might do business with us. Prayer is the very engine room for spiritual shaping and growth.

SCRIPTURE TO CONSIDER: Exod. 24:9–18; Zech. 4:8–14; Matt. 17:1–13; Heb. 12:18–29.

AN ACTION TO TAKE: Be sure to open your heart to God in your sacred space and prepare for wind, earthquake and fire, as well as the 'still small voice' (v12, NKJV).

A PRAYER TO MAKE: 'Lord, shape me in my prayer times, in my Godspace. Amen.'

Why study with us?

 Integrating your faith and your studies: Your faith isn't reserved for Sundays and church. It's part of who you are, and how you live out your profession. All of our courses are underpinned by a Christian ethos and understanding. Be encouraged to integrate your faith into your course, and your professional life beyond.

 Flexibility to suit your circumstances: Squeezing in study around your job, your family, and your 101 other responsibilities? We'll make it as easy as possible for you. You can enrol on a course that's taught part-time or online via distance education. We have campuses in Farnham and in Bradford to serve the south and the north of England.

 Choose your level: Whether you're studying for the first time, or you're a seasoned academic, you'll find a course at the level that suits you. You can try an introductory course, study a Waverley Award, or delve into a Masters, and anything in between.

 Tutors you can trust: Our tutors have years of experience in their fields and many have completed doctoral level studies. You'll hear our tutors on podcasts, or see them contributing to journals and academic discussion. You're learning from the highly-learned.

 Learning in community: Join a cohort of like-minded people and be part of the community of learners. Whether you're learning online or in-person, you'll be in touch regularly with your fellow students.

Where you can study

Our vision is to equip people, wherever they're based geographically. That's why we offer courses delivered in the Farnham Campus, Bradford Campus and via distance education.

Farnham Campus

Waverley Abbey House, Farnham, Surrey

Come on site to study any of the courses in the Counselling and Spiritual Formation Faculties.

Bradford Campus

Church on the Way, Bradford

You can study these counselling courses on site in Bradford:

- Introduction to Christian Care and Counselling

- Waverley Certificate in Christian Counselling

- Diploma of Higher Education in Counselling

Distance Education

Study from anywhere in the world with our courses delivered via distance education:

- Contemporary Chaplaincy

- Undergraduate Certificate / diploma in Integrating Faith and Leadership*

- Postgraduate MA in Public Leadership* *subject to validation

For more information on courses you can study, please visit
waverleyabbeycollege.ac.uk

1 Chronicles 17:7–15

'I declare to you that the LORD will build a house for you: when your days are over and you go to be with your ancestors, I will raise up your offspring to succeed you, one of your own sons, and I will establish his kingdom.' (vv10b–11)

Our prayer is limited by our mortality. We see in part only (1 Cor. 12:9—10), whilst God is the beginning and end of all (Rev. 22:13). So our prayer is constrained by the limitations of our earthbound vision and understanding. Here King David is restrained in his ambition to build God's house. Whilst the ambition is indeed godly, the timing for its execution lies in the future. This is not something for David, but for his successor. Our instincts can be right, yet without the seasoning of God's Spirit we may act outside of God's eternal purpose.

Prayer, individually and collectively, is essential to ensure that we are collaborating with God's Spirit in realising His purpose. In our age of personality, where image and branding appear to offer the substance of the promise, we are in danger of building castles in the sky that have no enduring legacy within God's call. David accepts Nathan's intervention and humbles himself before God, aware that the future lies in His hands alone. David is simply a momentary instrument in God's plan. It is with humility that we are to approach God's throne in prayer, mindful that our only significance lies in the degree to which we are yielded to God. As Isaac the Syrian said, 'The highest form of prayer is to stand silently in awe before God'.* Through prayer we make ourselves available to God, and submit our instincts to serve God's purpose in our life and work.

SCRIPTURE TO CONSIDER: Deut. 6:4–19; Jer. 23:25–32; John 9:1–12; Acts 20:25–38.

AN ACTION TO TAKE: How do you react to the word humility? Can you practise humility in daily life in your relationship with others?

A PRAYER TO MAKE: 'Lord, When I want to be first teach me how to be a willing servant of all. Amen.' (Mark 9:35)

* hilarion Alfeyev, 'The Spiritual World of Isaac the Syrian' (Kalamazoo, 2000)

1 Chronicles 29:10–14
**'Yours, LORD, is the greatness and the power and the
glory and the majesty and the splendour, for everything
in heaven and earth is yours. Yours, LORD, is the
kingdom; you are exalted as head over all.' (v11)**

We are constrained by mortal limitations but can ensure we
lay a solid foundation for the next generation who choose to
serve God. This is not legacy as a monument to ourselves but a
commitment to commissioning others for future kingdom-building. It's
a missional provision for the ongoing work of God. Our contribution
is made within our lifetime alone; our legacy is the extent to which we
equip others for success, a success for which God alone gets the glory.
Not a popular concept in our present-day, personality-shaped culture.

King David's prayer is in response to the generosity of God's people
in affording Solomon the means to realise God's calling on his life. This
prayer, reminiscent of the Lord's Prayer, reminds us that prayer is to be
populated with thanksgiving to God for the simple truth of His grace
and mercy. We shall never run out of praises for our God. Of course,
one way we can demonstrate our thanks is to invest in God's work
that will continue long after we are laid to rest. Today, Waverley Abbey
Trust continues as a ministry simply because of the faithful, prayerful
and financial investment in the anointed vision to equip and empower
people-helpers that Selwyn Hughes cast. The students who are now
working as counsellors, chaplains, and who minister throughout
society, are the fruit of the legacy of those faithful stewards who have
supported Waverley Abbey Trust. We work, pray and give to invest in
the future of God's mission from here.

SCRIPTURE TO CONSIDER: Gen. 2:4–17; Matt. 6:19–34; 2 Cor. 9:6–15; 1 Pet. 4:1–11.

AN ACTION TO TAKE: In what ways are you focused on supporting God's purpose
beyond your own lifetime? One way is to support Waverley Abbey Trust as
we equip others for Christian witness and service.

A PRAYER TO MAKE: 'Lord, may I always look to Your interests and not my own.
Amen.'

2 Chronicles 7:13–18

'If my people, who are called by my name, will humble themselves and pray and seek my face and turn from their wicked ways, then I will hear from heaven, and I will forgive their sin and will heal their land.' (v14)

Prayer is always about putting God first. We live in an age obsessed with itself. Fascinated with self-realisation and psychometrics, delving ever deeper into our assumed personality, it's easy to think that the world's future benefit has something to do with me. Whilst it may, it's not perhaps as much as we'd like to think. John the Baptist had the right understanding: our 'I' must decrease to make room for a growing awareness of God's presence and reality (John 3:30). The steps that lead us into prayer are simple; to know the life and lordship of Jesus and to submit to His rule. This is the heart attitude we must adopt if we are to approach God.

The objective of prayer is twofold. God hears our prayers and consistently forgives our many sins, the waywardness that seeks constantly to distract us from contemplating God and serving His will with our lives. Second, we carry responsibility that through our prayers we are consistently seeking to see the healing of the world in which we live. This is a critical part of our Christian service on earth, looking to God for wholeness throughout society, both in the UK and globally. God's invitation includes us all, since we need to travel no further than to our knees to secure God's purpose on earth. Consistent prayer captures God's attention and fertilises the earth in preparation for a harvest of godliness. It is the greatest contribution any of us can make.

SCRIPTURE TO CONSIDER: Isa. 55:1–11; Jer. 29:1–9; Acts 4:23–31; 1 Pet. 5:1–11.

AN ACTION TO TAKE: Either as a group or individually sign up for the e-learning course on *The Prayers of Jesus* with Amy Boucher Pye. Visit edwj.org/mj22-20may

A PRAYER TO MAKE: 'Lord, I choose to submit to You in every thought, word and action, and pray for the healing of the nations. Amen.'

Ezra 10:1–4

'While Ezra was praying and confessing, weeping and throwing himself down before the house of God, a large crowd of Israelites – men, women and children – gathered round him. They too wept bitterly.' (v1)

Ezra had returned to Jerusalem from exile in Babylon under strict instructions from its king, Artaxerxes. He was to establish the Temple and teach God's ways once more to the Israelites (Ezra 7). Discovering disobedience, Ezra humbled himself and prayed on behalf of those who faced God's judgment (Ezra 9). This illustrates how we can take responsibility to stand and pray before God on behalf of those whose actions deny God's truth (intercession). Ezra did not engage in dialogue with anyone but immediately turned to prayer. We live in an age of 24/7 news and comment, when often our first response is a social media post or retweeting something we 'like'. This leads to a crescendo of internet noise, highlighting disagreements and escalating division. As disciples we are invited to turn to private, personal prayer.

All who follow Jesus are encouraged to become 'first responders'. Our emergency service is prayer, and we are to prioritise this over everything. We may feel disengaged from the events unfolding around us in real time, be they sudden or slow-burning, but in fact we're involved in the heat of the battle and prayer influences outcomes in ways we cannot fully comprehend. That's because prayer is born of obedience and, as those who choose to obey God, we do not need to understand through the exercise of our reason, but of our faith. Faith is our distinctiveness in a world that proposes many solutions, the majority of which have borne little lasting fruit.

SCRIPTURE TO CONSIDER: Dan. 9:1–19; Hab. 1:1–4; 3:17–19; Luke 19:37–48; Rom. 9:1–18.

AN ACTION TO TAKE: Are you able to resist the temptation to add your voice to the cacophony of online comment and instead quietly humble yourself and pray?

A PRAYER TO MAKE: 'Lord, I can't go back and change the beginning, but I can start where I am and pray for Your will to be done here and around the world. Amen.'

Jesus Intercedes

Zechariah 1:12–17
'Therefore this is what the LORD says: "I will return to Jerusalem with mercy, and there my house will be rebuilt. And the measuring line will be stretched out over Jerusalem," declares the LORD Almighty.' (v16)

Whilst we have little knowledge of how prayer works in practice, here God's angel encourages Israel through Zechariah. We feel pressure when we pray. Life's problems close in, and we experience little by way of relief. Prayer requires courage and perseverance, for it is born of faith – unseen yet substantial (Heb. 11:1). Prayer can feel like emptying our words out into a bottomless void, with neither answer nor echo from their landing anywhere. This confirms that prayer is always faith acting on God's faithfulness. The angel here is, as so often in the OT, a representation of Christ. His words confirm that God is observant yet intervenes and acts according to His will and purpose alone. We find encouragement because we don't pray alone. Christ intercedes alongside us standing before God (Heb. 7:25). Prayer will feel a lonely and isolated space and we may choose to avoid it. Also we grow frustrated when continuous prayer apparently produces no measurable results. Yet, we're participating in the unseen dissonance that operates on the far horizon of our mortal understanding, a place where God works His purpose out. God is forever, whilst our lives flourish and fail within a few decades. We're invited to participate in God's purpose, yet often, like Abraham, the father of faith, we won't see the realisation of His promise (Heb. 11:13). Our temptation is to become distracted by our material world, the physical and tangible rather than the immaterial and spiritual. By God's grace we straddle both, and prayer composes the bridge between the two.

SCRIPTURE TO CONSIDER: Ps. 103:13–22; Isa. 11:1–9; Rom. 8:18–39; Eph. 6:10–20.

AN ACTION TO TAKE: Write down the things that you struggle with when you think about prayer. Is there someone you trust that you can talk these through with?

A PRAYER TO MAKE: 'Lord, help me to continue faithful in prayer, even when I feel like I am simply talking to myself. Amen.'

1 John 5:11–15

'This is the confidence we have in approaching God: that if we ask anything according to his will, he hears us. And if we know that he hears us – whatever we ask – we know that we have what we asked of him.' (vv14–15)

I love Andrew Murray's book *With Christ in the School of Prayer* because prayer is the product of learning. It's why I serve Waverley Abbey Trust's mission of both helping everyone learn how to live every day with Jesus, and equipping people through practical courses with the skills to serve others. It's taken time to discover how to pray within God's will. In simple terms God's will is self-evident for God desires that people turn to Christ and enjoy fullness of life (John 10:10). It will also teach us through life experience how to deepen our friendship with God and serve His kingdom purpose with our lives.

Often we can't be certain of the specifics of God's will, but we do know the broad parameters, and these are what we start with. So my morning prayers will include petitions for the Church, political leadership, my spiritual leaders, family and friends, and those in need such as people experiencing poverty. I know God wants to provide for all these wants, and sometimes the answer to our prayers lies within the lifestyles we choose to adopt, individually and as church congregations. Prayer is less about my own needs (which in reality are covered by others as they pray for my welfare) than the obvious needs of those I see around me. What can take time to learn is to step beyond the primacy of my own felt concerns and to serve the needs of others, just as Jesus showed us through His incarnation, ministry and death.

SCRIPTURE TO CONSIDER: Ps. 91:9–16; Zech. 13:7–9; Luke 11:9–13; John 16:19–28.

AN ACTION TO TAKE: Are you learning in God's school of prayer? What have been the most difficult lessons?

A PRAYER TO MAKE: 'Lord, I place my confidence in You and know that You hear and answer my prayers. Amen.'

Ephesians 1:15–23
**'I keep asking that the God of our Lord Jesus Christ, the
glorious Father, may give you the Spirit of wisdom and
revelation, so that you may know him better. I pray that the
eyes of your heart may be enlightened in order that you may
know the hope to which he has called you' (vv17–18)**

We are comfortable using our natural senses to make judgments. We observe, draw conclusions and make decisions based on our preconceptions. Paul prays that we might learn through the Spirit to have the eyes of our heart opened. Once again we are drawn into the reality of that which lies beyond our natural reach. God finds us, reveals the gospel and we choose if we shall respond (1 Cor. 15:1–5). Now we begin to see through the eyes of faith and life is not what it might at first appear. Also the cultural norms we have accepted may need challenging for they fail to serve God's interests and may threaten our own development as His disciple. We can place confidence in what we discern, yet we must learn to live in a world in which we live as 'resident aliens'. Our home is in another kingdom, and we are its ambassadors throughout our short stay on the earth.

We start each day with prayer for it is the threshold on which we open our spiritual eyes and ask God that we might see all that He is doing around us. The self-evident is seldom born of the Spirit. It takes a devoted disciple to learn to live dependent on God's leading, and to develop the eye of faith. Finding hope, the will of God, in our daily life experience is always a challenge but this is the Christian life, learning more of God daily whilst investing ourselves in God's purposes.

SCRIPTURE TO CONSIDER: 2 Cor. 4:1–18; Acts 26:1–19; Phil. 3:15–21; 1 Pet. 2:1–17.

AN ACTION TO TAKE: Learning to see through the eye of faith is how we discover God's way in the world in which we live.

A PRAYER TO MAKE: 'Lord, teach me to see through Your eyes and present You to those I meet every day. Amen.'

John 17:13–19
**'My prayer is not that you take them out of the world
but that you protect them from the evil one. They are
not of the world, even as I am not of it.' (vv15–16)**

Whilst Christians are citizens of heaven, their sphere of
influence is in the world. Indeed, the discipleship is to provide
evidence to an unbelieving world of the truth of the gospel
of salvation through Jesus. Too often, fear of the world has created
an inwardlooking church, more engaged with its own wellbeing and
preservation than following in Jesus' footsteps and willing to leave the
familiar in response to God's call to explore what we don't yet know.
Again, too often, mission is reduced to activities held by the church and
in surroundings with which the church is comfortable, under the false
expectation that people are interested in meeting God on church terms.

The Church was born out of persecution and, fearing the challenge
of a secularised world today, faces the temptation to compromise
with prevailing cultures. Whilst Jesus does not invite us to create
conflict, itself a barrier to the gospel, we are equally not to surrender
to an unbiblical understanding of the world and humanity's place and
purpose within it. The gospel turns on the life, death and resurrection
of Jesus, and we must continue to explain this gospel of hope,
regardless of all opposition. Many today are dissatisfied with the
place secular humanism has brought the world to. Christians retain
a strong proposition, a worldview that gives purpose and a generous
and inclusive sense of direction for everyone. As such, we are to retain
confidence in the gospel, and refuse to reduce its meaning and power
to serve the interests of rationality.

SCRIPTURE TO CONSIDER: Ezek. 13:17–23; John 3:16–36; 1 Cor. 10:23–33; Eph.
5:1–20.

AN ACTION TO TAKE: Do you have confidence in the gospel of Jesus? You may
not feel confident in having answers, but you are invited to live faithfully in
the world you serve.

A PRAYER TO MAKE: 'Lord, help me to share a piece of heaven with everyone I
meet every day. Amen.'

Living Sacrifice

Romans 12:1–3

'Do not conform to the pattern of this world, but be transformed by the renewing of your mind. Then you will be able to test and approve what God's will is – his good, pleasing and perfect will.' (v2)

W e're no longer who we were once we've encountered and accepted Christ. Change is evident, and many testify to differences others noticed about them after they converted to Christianity. Grace begins a work of sanctification within us, by which we grow to become more like Jesus (Matt. 5:48). However, this change is gradual. Like a stag loses its antlers each year, and the resultant new growth reveals its maturity, so we daily pursue God in prayer that we might also grow in understanding and Christian maturity. Through humble obedience we are invited to flourish in our formation in Christ, and the Spirit Himself heals our brokenness.

Of course, it is in the place of prayer that we give our full attention to God and here that much of His healing work takes place. Shut in with the Spirit, we grasp both our total need of God and perceive all clutter that distances us from Him. Here we have an opportunity to call on God's help in demolishing all those barriers that obstruct us from reaching God's intimacy. This transformation is preparing us for an eternity with God, and transcends the attractive, yet short-lived, delights, all that mortal life can offer us. They may appear to present immediate gratification, but leave nothing but a memory of a momentary pleasure. This is our daily battle, what Paul describes as 'living sacrifice'. It will cost us, demand an act of the will and reveal the level of our devotion to God. What do we want?

SCRIPTURE TO CONSIDER: Ezek. 36:22–32; 2 Cor. 5:11–21; 1 Pet. 1:13–25; 1 John 2:1–6.

AN ACTION TO TAKE: Do you desire to become a living sacrifice for God? What immediate steps do you need to take?

A PRAYER TO MAKE: 'Lord, help me to seek maturity in Christ and to cooperate with Your Spirit. Amen.'

Write to micha@edwj.org and I'll write back personally and in confidence as soon as I can.

Be Fervent in Prayer

Romans 12:9–13

'Never be lacking in zeal, but keep your spiritual fervour, serving the Lord. Be joyful in hope, patient in affliction, faithful in prayer.' (vv11–12)

One challenge with prayer is that we too easily lose interest and gently drift from our commitment to God. The cause may be found in our disappointment in God's response to our prayer or, more often, the busyness of life. Prayer can appear drab in comparison with the many other opportunities life presents to us. Time is limited and space with God is all too easily abandoned. Yet, God inhabits the wilderness of our lives, those spaces where we independently cultivate our own crops in an attempt to feed ourselves. God is always present with us even when we lose sight of Him. We may confess a love for God, yet zeal alone can inspire that love to action and deepen our desire for Him.

Paul identifies the three key distinctives of the disciple as joy, patience and faithful prayer. Life on earth is not easy with its many challenges, disappointments and trials. Yet, as we deepen our friendship, and grow in our confidence, we find hope in the darkest experiences, enduring afflictions that raise questions and deeply impact how we can live life. These will always test our commitment to prayer, when they appear to go unheard. All we have to hand is God's promise and we question if this is sufficient. Each of us will need to determine this answer for ourselves. Yet, it is in these places that we demonstrate that prayer can sustain us and reveal, to our surprise, that God's grace is sufficient for us in the reality of life.

SCRIPTURE TO CONSIDER: Ps. 62:1–8; 2 Cor. 12:1–10; Col. 4:2–6; Heb. 10:26–39.

AN ACTION TO TAKE: Are there experiences that have challenged your commitment to pray? How, and with whom, do you deal with the questions this provokes?

A PRAYER TO MAKE: 'Lord, please continually hold me by my hand and guide me through my life. Amen.' (See Ps. 73:21–26.)

Write to micha@edwj.org and I'll write back personally and in confidence as soon as I can.

Ask and Believe

James 1:2–8
**'But when you ask, you must believe and not doubt,
because the one who doubts is like a wave of the sea,
blown and tossed by the wind. That person should not
expect to receive anything from the Lord.' (vv6–7)**

James' message is simple because God's way is simple but as humans we lean towards complexity. We constantly make mountains out of molehills. God's way (Matt. 5:48) is plain but we insist on complicating it with both reason and sinfulness. There's a lot that competes for our allegiance, and God invites us to make our choices for He's no enforcer. When we simplify our approach and live God's way our reward is the 'crown of life' (James 1:12). Taking hold of this crown is a disciple's life's ambition. However, ambition costs nothing; only its realisation demands total attention and maximum effort. We need constantly to ask ourselves, what distracts us from our godly ambition?

Many times we've noted that faith operates in the realm of the unseen. It is a promise, which is only partially fulfilled within our mortal experience. It can only be fully realised once we pass across death's threshold, one reason death need hold no fears for us, only for those we leave behind and who grieve our loss. So we are faced daily with this question; am I motivated more by what I can see, experience and touch, or by God's promise – unseen, unfelt and immaterial? This is why our will is the most important aspect of our personhood when it comes to pursuing God. And our will is nurtured and nourished through prayer, for it alone offers the difference between success and failure in our walk of faith.

SCRIPTURE TO CONSIDER: 1 Kings 18:16–21; Isa. 29:11–16; Matt. 21:18–22; Eph. 4:11–16.

AN ACTION TO TAKE: How do you wrestle with the simple message of Scripture? What prevents you from remaining single-minded, day in and day out?

A PRAYER TO MAKE: 'Lord, strengthen the resolve of my will to follow You faithfully and completely in every sphere of my life. Amen.'

James 4:1–6
'When you ask, you do not receive, because you ask with wrong motives, that you may spend what you get on your pleasures. You adulterous people, don't you know that friendship with the world means enmity against God?' (vv3–4a)

We face a human dilemma. God says He answers our prayers on many occasions in Scripture, yet some of our prayers appear to go unanswered. We also appreciate that they need to be in agreement with God's unseen purpose. God's character is revealed throughout Scripture, and we, like the Israelites throughout the OT, learn more of that character daily through experience. There's a danger that we project human emotions and characteristics onto God. We assume He understands the human condition in the way we do, yet God isn't subject to our emotions and anxieties. When Luke records Jesus resolutely embracing His execution (9:51) we get a glimpse of the resolution we need to follow Jesus in order to sustain and grow our faith and reveal God's kingdom.

When praying, we easily ask from wrong motives. We naturally want to avoid pain and loss but our prayer is best focused on the global tragedies that unfold daily. We see highly qualified, now impoverished refugees floating up on Britain's shores. What's our reaction? Before ever looking for a political solution, we are to fall to our knees and pray. We are to recall that their experience may become our experience, and we will then become dependent on the prayers of the global Church to sustain us in desperate circumstances. When our prayers centre on our own desires primarily, we pray amiss. We are to bring our concerns together with the needs of others, our motive that God's will is done.

SCRIPTURE TO CONSIDER: Prov. 1:28–33; Isa. 1:10–17; Matt. 21:18–22; Eph. 4:11–16.

AN ACTION TO TAKE: What have you learnt about God's character and how does it influence your decision-making?

A PRAYER TO MAKE: 'Lord, I come, pray and listen to You. I seek You with all my heart and I know that You are here with me. Amen.'

Fast and Pray

Matthew 6:16–18

'But when you fast, put oil on your head and wash your face, so that it will not be obvious to others that you are fasting, but only to your Father, who is unseen; and your Father, who sees what is done in secret, will reward you.' (vv17–18)

The good we do in obedience to God runs the risk of becoming a source for our own self-promotion and gratification. Self-congratulation, encouraged by the praise of others, is a temptation we all face. We desire affirmation for the things we do. However, anonymity is taught by Jesus (Luke 5:14). God's work is clear only to those with eyes and ears to see and hear it. This is not for some hidden, mystical purpose but because learning the ways of God is the product of faithful and devoted discipleship. Whilst God's kingdom is open to all, He recognises human capacity for self-deceit; we so easily assume the applause and recognition we receive is due to our ability. We fail to step aside and allow God all the glory.

Whilst it appears an impossibility to conceal what we are doing, as in fasting and giving (Matt. 6:3–4), when we become known for such things we run a great risk. In our society many people seek to make names for themselves. This feeds human vanity and can guarantee financial success. However, God knowing our weakness in such areas warns us to go about our spiritual formation quietly, determined to remain as invisible as possible. Whatever we do in God's service we should keep between us and God; yet we are to appear healthy and whole, as this speaks well to others of the love and care of the God we worship.

SCRIPTURE TO CONSIDER: Isa. 58:1–9; Jer. 5:18–31; Matt. 13:10–17; Luke 14:1–14.

AN ACTION TO TAKE: One of the greatest challenges is to choose to be anonymous. Is it sufficient to be fully known by God alone?

A PRAYER TO MAKE: 'Lord, teach me to fast in quietness and to serve You without seeking human recognition. Amen.'

Spiritual Formation

Spiritual Formation students at Waverley Abbey College grow in their understanding of who God made them to be and they become equipped to help others on their spiritual journeys.

Strengthen Your Core

In Search of Friendship

"Learning spiritual formation has broadened my concept of the heavenly Father and strengthened my faith by challenging what I believe God is doing in every part of life. God is good and this course helps us see our spiritual life more clearly."

Steve

For more information on our spiritual formation resources and courses please visit our websites

Resources – wvly.org/cl

Courses – wvly.org/sf-overview

Send Out Workers

Matthew 9:35–38
'Then he said to his disciples, "The harvest is plentiful but
the workers are few. Ask the Lord of the harvest, therefore,
to send out workers into his harvest field."' (vv37–38)

Tomorrow we move from prayer to mission. The two are intimately linked since mission is born from prayer. Indeed, as we mission we also pray. Mission is God's love shared in a broken world. We pray for workers to go out and reap a harvest of those hungry for God's grace. This request appears to suggest numerical increase, yet Jesus didn't rapidly expand His team. So it's best understood as a prayer for each disciple to become more engaged in carrying the gospel to family, friends, neighbours and colleagues. For as our godly love and service grows, so we seek to invite others to meet with the risen Lord.

One way we can put our faith to work in the different spheres of society is by training as a chaplain. The word itself is drawn from an incident involving a Roman soldier, Martin of Tours. Around 337 in Amiens, France, he noticed a poor man in rags and drew his sword to divide his military cloak in half and gave one half to a shivering beggar in the freezing cold. *capella* is the Latin for 'little cloak'. The role of the chaplain is to share what they have with someone in need. At Waverley Abbey College we run a one-year, part-time, online course designed to equip those serving, or looking to serve, in a broad range of community or church-based settings to prepare people for practical and effective mission. Full- or part-time, this is a great form of mission.

SCRIPTURE TO CONSIDER: Ps. 121; 126:3–6; John 14:1–21; Col. 2:6–15.

AN ACTION TO TAKE: Is it time for you or someone you know to train as a chaplain? For details visit edwj.org/mj22-31may

A PRAYER TO MAKE: 'Lord, teach me to share what I have found in God generously with others as I embark on mission. Amen.'

Write to micha@edwj.org and I'll write back personally and in confidence as soon as I can.

Send Out Workers

Luke 4:16–21

'The Spirit of the Lord is on me, because he has anointed me to proclaim good news to the poor. He has sent me to proclaim freedom for the prisoners and recovery of sight for the blind, to set the oppressed free, to proclaim the year of the Lord's favour.' (vv18–19)

If we're serious in our quest to love and serve Jesus, then we'd best start with Jesus' chosen mission. He takes these stirring promises from the prophet Isaiah and makes them His mission mandate. There are two clear meanings here. First, He describes those who are entrapped in sin and cannot see spiritual reality. Consequently, they are prisoners to their spiritual poverty and gospel deficit. We were first found by God in this condition and our eyes were opened to our gospel need, and, like the emperor's new clothes, we discovered we were naked whilst deceived into thinking we were fully dressed.

Second, Jesus addresses the harsh realities of those identified in His mandate. As we journey with the Gospel writers we see miracles, each one a sign of Jesus' divine authority to silence His critics with a message of love and hope. Our prayers always carry the needs of our world to God. At the same time we are commissioned by God and equipped by the Holy Spirit to engage in meeting the needs of others and, like Jesus, offering hope to those feeling lost in a confusing world. The only evidence we carry is our testimony of God's truth as experienced in our lives. Such testimony can only be known when we dare to communicate it. Mission is bringing others the story of God's grace that we have experienced in our own life. We always carry this treasure within us, always available for the people we meet along the way.

SCRIPTURE TO CONSIDER: Gen. 12:1–9; Isa. 61; Mark 3:1–6; Rom. 10:5–15.

AN ACTION TO TAKE: Take some time to think of ways that you know God has met you in your life. This is your testimony. Ready to share it with others?

A PRAYER TO MAKE: 'Lord, help me to prepare my testimony so that I might serve Jesus' mission mandate every day. Amen.'

Into the World

John 17:13–19
**'As you sent me into the world, I have sent them
into the world. For them I sanctify myself, that
they too may be truly sanctified.' (vv18–19)**

Mission in the New Testament (NT) means 'to send' and implies
that we receive authority from the one who sends us. So, just
as Jesus was sent and enjoyed the Father's full authority,
here He prays for all of us to know the government of God in and
through our lives of obedient service. God's authority is dependent
on our obedience, one reason that it's so often and clearly stressed
throughout Scripture. In sanctifying us, Jesus dedicates us to God and
presents us as an offering to God. Whilst sin is dealt with once for all
on the cross, we are living sacrifices (Rom. 12:1) who offer ourselves
voluntarily for however God sees we might best express His kingdom
purpose. This is why every morning I prayerfully dedicate myself to
God and His mission.

Whilst we live in the world, we are not of the world – for the world
could never introduce us to God, nor to His 'wisdom, a mystery that
has been hidden and that God destined for our glory before time began'
(1 Cor 2:7). We're invited to take hold of this wisdom only revealed
through the Spirit, described as, 'What no eye has seen, what no
ear has heard, and what no human mind has conceived – the things
God has prepared for those who love him' (1 Cor. 2:9). We now have
confidence to speak this gospel mystery to an unbelieving world. The
challenge we always face is that we now understand as citizens of
heaven, no longer being earthbound.

SCRIPTURE TO CONSIDER: Ps. 30:6–12; Isa. 64:4–12; 1 Cor 2; 12:1–11.

AN ACTION TO TAKE: Have you ever given much thought to how in Christ you are
both dedicated to God whilst also a living sacrifice? Where is God asking
you to serve Him today?

A PRAYER TO MAKE: 'Lord, introduce me daily to Your word for this world so I
might prove a faithful servant. Amen.'

Acts 13:46–49
**'For this is what the Lord has commanded us: "I have made
you a light for the Gentiles, that you may bring salvation to
the ends of the earth." When the Gentiles heard this, they
were glad and honoured the word of the Lord; and all who
were appointed for eternal life believed.' (vv47–48)**

Christ's love compels us to share His message of hope and
wholeness for fractured humanity. God's first question was,
'Where are you?' (Gen. 3:9), the question that resounds throughout
every generation. Today's preoccupation with self and the ready
availability of so many self-help courses is testimony to the insecurity
that runs deep within the human heart. God's message of salvation,
revealed through the ministry of Jesus, is the profound response to inert
human angst. There is a peace that passes all rational explanations
available in God's good news (Phil. 4:7). This hope and wholeness is
available to all who turn to Jesus. All God requires is an agreement to
explore His paths, and we can begin to resolve the anxieties that so
often imprison the human heart. Just like light, God's revelation reveals
the landscape of our life and we are able to make choices about what
we will do and who we want to become. Written deep within our heart
from our conception, God places within our hands the tools required
to clean up our act and live in service of the one who created us. The
process following our surrender to God is to honour God's Word in the
way we choose to live our life. We now look to God and seek to serve
others, God's two greatest commands (Matt 22:34–40). Remarkably,
Christianity invites everyone to consider living the God-life. There are
no barriers to entry – we are all struggling sinners.

SCRIPTURE TO CONSIDER: 2 Pet. 3:3–9; Isa. 25:1–9; John 1:9–18; Acts 3:17–26.

AN ACTION TO TAKE: Have you made your peace with God and found grace to
quell the anxieties of life? How do you manage when things begin to get on
top of you?

A PRAYER TO MAKE: 'Lord, light up the dark corners of my life so that I can invite
Your Spirit to renew me by Your grace. Amen.'

1 Chronicles 16:23–30

'Sing to the LORD, all the earth; proclaim his salvation day after day. Declare his glory among the nations, his marvellous deeds among all peoples. For great is the LORD and most worthy of praise; he is to be feared above all gods.' (vv23–25)

O ur missional message applies to the whole world. God is creator and Lord of all, for nothing can exist without God. Indeed, time itself is dependent on God's word, ending at His command. Whilst we must consider and contend with many conflicting worldviews in deciding what we want to believe, we can place full confidence in God's revelation. That confidence is something we choose to embrace in part, whilst it's also dependent on God's grace sustaining us. Where we meet situations we don't understand we entrust them to God, and so demonstrate our faith in action. In a world in which opinion is strongly expressed across myriad channels, our responsibility is to wait on God and serve His purpose.

There is a danger that we can lose confidence in the power of God's Word, the Bible, which we may struggle to understand. In the first century AD, whilst the first Christians enjoyed access to the Hebrew Bible (our OT), the first attempt at an authoritative NT was the Muratorian Canon around AD 200.* It was not until the fifth century that all the different Christian churches came to a basic agreement on biblical canon. We can place our confidence in the work of the early church fathers who agreed to what amounts to the Bible today, and we can have confidence in it as a source for guiding how we both think and live. We can never live the Christian life without Scripture to guide us.

SCRIPTURE TO CONSIDER: James 1:22–27; Ps. 119:105–120; Col. 1:15–23; 2 Tim. 3:10–17.

AN ACTION TO TAKE: Does Scripture answer your life questions? *Search the Scriptures* uses a question-and-answer approach, and helps you discover God's truth for yourself. edwj.org/mj22-4jun2

A PRAYER TO MAKE: 'Lord, help me to understand Your word and walk in Your footsteps every day in understanding and practice. Amen.'

* edwj.org/mj22-4jun [accessed 13/02/2022]

Let the Earth Rejoice

Psalm 96:11–13
'Let all creation rejoice before the LORD, for he
comes, he comes to judge the earth.
He will judge the world in righteousness and
the peoples in his faithfulness.' (v13)

L ife slides by at its own pace. Demanding daily schedules mean we
can feel we haven't time to breathe. The older I get the faster time
passes, but I also become more aware of my mortality. My end
was always in my beginning; now, with some excitement, I can almost
taste that end. I'm acutely aware of my opportunities to live good news
in my neighbourhood and with family and colleagues. Scripture reveals
a world in harmony with itself, with every element giving praise to God.
Indeed, Jesus reminded us that when *we* won't praise then the *stones*
will break forth in song (Luke 19:37–40).

God is the creator of all and we know that creation itself groans
under the weight of expectation of Christ's return (Rom. 8:22–23). In the
familiarity of the every day it's easy to lose sight of the fact that Christ
is returning. Consequently, we get stuck in the immediate and forget
that our lives are invested in a project initiated by the incarnate Christ.
When we feel stuck or dispirited, let's recall that everything around us
reflects the source of our life. Walking around the streets or through
the woods, we have many reasons to lift our voices in praise of God.
This has the power to lift us from our own despondency and also lifts
the weight of responsibility from our shoulders. It is God's vision we
serve and God carries the responsibility. We are privileged to briefly
participate in that vision of declaring God's glory with our every breath.

SCRIPTURE TO CONSIDER: Isa. 42:1–9; 55:12–13; Rom. 1:18–32; 2 Tim. 3:10–17.

AN ACTION TO TAKE: Have you considered your life in the light of Christ's return?
What impact does this have on your thinking?

A PRAYER TO MAKE: 'Lord, as I look at the wonders of Your creation I choose to
sing a song of praise in awe of Your creative wisdom. Amen.'

Write to micha@edwj.org and I'll write back personally and in confidence as soon as I can.

Power to Serve

Acts 1:6–10

'But you will receive power when the Holy Spirit comes on you; and you will be my witnesses in Jerusalem, and in all Judea and Samaria, and to the ends of the earth.' (v8)

As disciples of Jesus and embracing His call to mission, the great news is that we need not depend on our own abilities. The power, or simply the capability to *be* good news, is given by God through the Holy Spirit. Coming from God, it carries His authority. Authority and ability are entrusted to us as God's ambassadors on earth to serve the purpose of God on earth. Too often, this great gift has been dissipated in a beneficial side-show offering benefits within the church, yet failing to find expression in the majority of our life beyond the church building's boundary wall. Mission means 'send' and, like Jesus' extraordinary example, we too are expected to learn to live and serve God in an unfamiliar and fast-changing culture. Jesus goes to the margins with His message; so must we.

Once beyond the boundaries of church-orchestrated meetings, we can feel uncertain, even fearful, about owning, let alone explaining, our faith. So we must ask ourselves how confident are we in our God? We can never persuade anyone to respond to Jesus' invitation of eternal life, nor are we asked to. We are simply to be witnesses, or martyrs! It's encouraging that Origen said, 'The Saviour gives the name of martyr to everyone who bears witness to the truth'.* So we are all martyrs. Whilst it may not lead to our physical death, it will require that we die to self, as Jesus clearly stated.

SCRIPTURE TO CONSIDER: Luke 9:21–27; John 12:23–28; Gal. 2:11–21; 2 Tim. 1:3–14.

AN ACTION TO TAKE: A martyr is simply a witness. What does your life give witness to? Is this a representation of God's love?

A PRAYER TO MAKE: 'Lord, may I learn to live neither through my natural strength or ability but by Your Spirit in all I think, say and do. Amen.'

*Origen's Commentary on John, Book II. In *The Ante-Nicene Fathers, Volume IX.* chap. 28

John 20:19–22
'Again Jesus said, "Peace be with you! As the Father has sent me, I am sending you."' (v21)

This brief sentence carries a lot of weight. Jesus commissions, or entrusts, His disciples with delegated authority to go out and share the gospel with the world. Their mission is no different from that committed to Jesus by His Father. Indeed, the Church inherits Jesus' call to make disciples throughout the world. This forms the basis for Jesus' final instructions to His disciples following His resurrection. This commission is passed on to all the disciples equally and so we share responsibility today to realise this same commission, acting as faithful, and faith-filled, guides in a confused world. This is not something we aspire to or determine for ourselves; this is something that is bestowed on us by God's own hand (Heb. 5:4).

We must ask ourselves a simple question. Whom did Jesus serve? As He chose to do the will of the Father, so we are invited to invest ourselves in serving God's will through our life on earth. Scripture promises fullness of joy, despite our anxiety that this might lead to a rather austere life. Establishing how this commission plays out in our lives is critical to making decisions. Jesus invites us to take up this responsibility for mission and join Him in revealing the grace of God on earth. We can feel overwhelmed and nervous, uncertain as to what this might lead to. Yet this is the same Jesus who promises His disciples 'fullness of life' (John 10:10). Surely this is what we seek from our brief mortal stay on earth.

SCRIPTURE TO CONSIDER: Isa. 63:1–10; Matt. 28:16–20; Luke 24:36–49; John 13:12–38.

AN ACTION TO TAKE: What does commission mean to you? As one who is sent, how do you work that out in your everyday life? Where are the challenges for you?

A PRAYER TO MAKE: 'Lord, thank You that I am ordained through Your Word and promise to live my life in Your service. Amen.'

Isaiah 52:5–7

'"Therefore my people will know my name; therefore in that day they will know that it is I who foretold it. Yes, it is I." How beautiful on the mountains are the feet of those who bring good news' (vv6–7a)

We've been sold an empty promise. Caricatured as the 'American Dream' (the belief that anyone might realise their highest aspirations and goals), it proves an empty aphorism for most. The phrase emerged in 1931, when the USA enjoyed competitive advantage over every other nation, and was coined in the book, *The Epic of America* by James Truslow Adams. He encouraged everyone to 'dream of a land in which life should be better and richer and fuller for everyone, with opportunity for each according to ability or achievement' regardless of social class or birth. It's self-evident that being born addicted to drugs through a parent's choice, displaced by war and unwanted by a majority of nations, or with a so-called physical disability, the dream is inaccessible to many.

We can channel our sense of exclusion into envy, anger and despair, or we can look to the kingdom dream substantiated by God. Here the promise is far more appealing. Love, acceptance and personal wellbeing. A quick look around the USA and other countries reveals that the American Dream is contradicted by the reality of the majority of people's lives. Good job God has no investment in the shallow benefits of personal peace and affluence. Rather, He challenges us to find faith, then joyfully share that faith with other strugglers. No cheap grace here, but a freedom both to know myself and find confidence in a life offering meaning through grace as well as the companionship of fellow disciples. We are rich in God's grace and love.

SCRIPTURE TO CONSIDER: Exod. 3:1–12; Ps. 74:9–23; Jer. 31:23–34; Heb. 6:13–20.

AN ACTION TO TAKE: What dream are you aspiring to? How focused are you on realising it?

A PRAYER TO MAKE: 'Lord, I rejoice that I am known by You and am a member of a caring, sharing and supportive family of faith-filled disciples. Amen.'

Jeremiah 1:1–10

'But the LORD said to me, "Do not say, 'I am too young.' You must go to everyone I send you to and say whatever I command you. Do not be afraid of them, for I am with you and will rescue you," declares the LORD.' (vv7–8)

Sometimes we're over eager to serve God in what we do. In my twenties with Youth for Christ, I mistook my youthful enthusiasm and zeal for the authority and strength of God. Six months of physical exhaustion followed at age 27. A hard lesson taught me by God. However, Jeremiah humbly responds, acknowledging concerns about his youthfulness. God encourages him, for when God calls it is neither age nor experience that counts, but the seal of God's approval. Until such time it is essential we remain faithful in the simple ways God requires, with hidden prayer, holy lifestyle and love of neighbour. This was Ananias' life, who was fearful yet obedient when God called him to pray for Saul's eyesight, and the apostle Paul was anointed as a result (Acts 9:10–19). God requests that we live faithful lives, never straining to do the work of God but quietly waiting, always available, for His call. Our endeavours cannot speed the coming of the kingdom, nor hasten Christ's return. They are more often the products of spiritual insecurity, providing us assurance that we are usefully serving God. We are to provide a consistent, often unnoticed, witness to God's presence in the world, our prayers encouraging the establishment of God's will in ways we may never see or understand. We are sent primarily to prove faithful in God's service – our mission. Occasionally God entrusts us with some specific task, and even if we feel inadequate in this, we shall find He has fully fitted us to complete it.

SCRIPTURE TO CONSIDER: Exod. 6:1–12; Isa. 6:1–11; Matt. 24:36–51; Acts 9:7–19.

AN ACTION TO TAKE: Are you content with being sent by God to engage in hidden prayer, holy lifestyle and love of neighbour? Is there a need to 'do something' for God? Why is that?

A PRAYER TO MAKE: 'Lord, enable me to be faithful in being consistent in my Christian life and available to respond to Your call if it comes. Amen.'

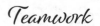

2 Timothy 2:1–10

'You then, my son, be strong in the grace that is in Christ Jesus. And the things you have heard me say in the presence of many witnesses entrust to reliable people who will also be qualified to teach others.' (vv1–2)

It's all too easy to think God's mission sits with me. Somehow my performance will make the difference between success and failure. Oh, that we carried such importance in the purpose of God. Our work is both to pray and love God, whilst collaborating with others to demonstrate the truth of the gospel. This is simply the announcement that Jesus died and rose again, is now with God, and invites us into relationship and to partner with the Trinity in serving God's interests on earth. Collaboration is essential since with different gifts we have a far greater reach across our community than if we operated alone. We also find encouragement as we learn from each other. The church is primarily the means by which such cooperation can best be organised to witness to the love of God throughout its local neighbourhood.

Discipleship cannot guarantee a pain-free life. In fact, we may be called on to suffer for the purpose of making God known. Yet, such suffering is to be measured against eternity, even though pain is acute in each moment of our suffering. Here we can look back over the witness of the Church since the Ascension of Christ and observe a long list of faithful servants who have walked this way before us. We are to draw encouragement and learn from our history, as well as our present. We carry the responsibility to continue the faithful witness of those who have gone before us, as well as to hand that tradition on to the generation that follows ours.

SCRIPTURE TO CONSIDER: Prov. 13:12–25; Mal. 2:1–10; 1 Cor. 4:1–13; Titus 2:7–15.

AN ACTION TO TAKE: How well do you collaborate with others? You will never build effectively on your own.

A PRAYER TO MAKE: 'Lord, help me to share my skills with others so we can build Your kingdom together. Amen.'

Luke 10:1–11

'Go! I am sending you out like lambs among wolves. Do not take a purse or bag or sandals; and do not greet anyone on the road.' (vv3–4)

C hristian life and witness is challenging. Lambs have a healthy regard for wolves who can easily destroy them. One reason Christianity is fragile in our world is that it does not have the ability to sustain itself. The source of all its power is in God. Jesus Himself is described as the Lamb of God (John 1:29) and reveals that He does not win through might and power, but through obedience to His Father in heaven (John 5:19). If Jesus is dependent on His Father, then it follows that we are in exactly the same position. We are not confrontational but our value is in the way we choose to live and to love. On all occasions, our speech refuses to escalate conflict or insult another (Col. 4:6).

If we are to find our way as disciples in what is often a hostile environment, we need to be determined in our decision to follow Jesus. As James tells us, if we are in two minds then circumstances will destabilise our confidence in God and in ourselves (James 1:8). We are also not to depend on our own resources but look to Jesus alone to meet our needs, moment by moment. A challenge to the depth of confidence we actually have in God. Finally, we are to seek to bring a blessing wherever we go. Such a blessing will either create a welcome or we will be swiftly rejected. God invites us to invest in those who receive our blessing.

SCRIPTURE TO CONSIDER: Ps. 22:19–28; Ezek. 2:3–10; John 15:18–25; Acts 14:21–28.

AN ACTION TO TAKE: What and who represents the wolves in your life? Be of good cheer, Christ has overcome the world (John 16:33).

A PRAYER TO MAKE: 'Lord, enable me to be faithful in being consistent in my Christian life, always available to respond to Your call if it comes. Amen.'

Write to micha@edwj.org and I'll write back personally and in confidence as soon as I can.

Fruitbearing

John 15:9–17
'You did not choose me, but I chose you and appointed you so that you might go and bear fruit – fruit that will last – and so that whatever you ask in my name the Father will give you. This is my command: love each other.' (vv16–17)

Vines take time to grow. As natural climbers they need support, and as we are grafted into Jesus the vine so we find the support our lives need to flourish. This support ensures the vine grows upright, and God intends that we learn to live upright lives. The vinedresser, who is our Father, carefully prunes it into shape, and ensures that the grapes are accessible whilst enjoying maximum light for ripening. Since vines can tolerate extreme conditions, they can produce a remarkable crop even with restricted access to water and nutrients. So as we live our life on earth, we are far more resilient than we may realise and can remain robust in harsh situations where there's little obvious support for the gospel.

Grapes all feed and grow on the one vine, and so Jesus stresses the need for Christian communities to love one another. We will always face differences in understanding but the gospel, as set out by Paul (Rom. 1:1–6), is the foundation upon which we can work together for God's purpose. Too often we create ghettos of glory, spend too much time disagreeing, whilst asserting that we alone embrace God's truth. When we fail to work together in the gospel, we confuse the world – whose view of Jesus is all too easily reduced to a series of scattered jigsaw pieces rather than a coherent picture of hope for all. Learning to love each other is critical to all effective missions.

SCRIPTURE TO CONSIDER: Deut. 10:14–22; Ezek. 18:1–12; 1 Cor. 13:4–13; 1 Pet. 4:1–11.

AN ACTION TO TAKE: Are you critical of other Christian disciples who are not part of your clan? Make a plan to talk to people beyond your immediate Christian circle and learn as you share in the gospel.

A PRAYER TO MAKE: 'Lord, may I remain grafted onto You and bear much fruit. Amen.'

Give to make a difference

Our Bible reading notes are read by hundreds of thousands of people around the world. *Every Day with Jesus* and *Inspiring Women Every Day* are now free in the UK. We want everyone, whatever their financial means to have access to these resources that help them walk each day with our Saviour.

It makes all the difference. One reader in Malaysia said:

When I was first exposed to Every Day with Jesus about two years ago, I could sense something different, something refreshing, and I was energised. I used to struggle to translate knowledge into my daily life. EDWJ helped me to be more insightful, more positive, and to enjoy everyday life as a disciple. This helps me to be patient and positive at home, at work, and at church.

As we trust in God's provision, we know there are costs to providing this ministry. Can you give to make a difference in someone's life? Could supporting this vision be a way in which you serve?

A gift of just £2 a month from you will put daily Bible reading notes into the hands of at least one person who is hungry to know God and experience His presence every day.

Visit **wvly.org/donate** to give to make a difference, or use the form at the back of these notes.

Exodus 7:1–6

**'But I will harden Pharaoh's heart, and though I multiply my
signs and wonders in Egypt, he will not listen to you. Then I will
lay my hand on Egypt and with mighty acts of judgment I will
bring out my divisions, my people the Israelites.' (vv3–4)**

Plunged into the cut and thrust of daily living we quickly lose
perspective on life. We can withdraw from what offends and
confuses us into a community that reinforces our own beliefs. Or
we can use Scripture to accommodate the prevailing cultural context
and social mores. Neither responses can reveal 'the goodness of the
LORD in the land of the living' (Ps. 27:13). Life is our greatest challenge to
confidence in God. We experience personal setbacks and see troubles
in the life experience of others. God is unchanging (Ps. 55:19) and
consequently we are invited to explore how His will is to be expressed in
serving the contemporary world.

Moses discovered that responding to God isn't the result of a
convincing argument or supernatural intervention. Faith is always a
choice which individuals can make, but equally reject. There is nothing
with which we can sweeten the pill of truth, for turning to God requires
me to submit myself to God entirely. I don't retain a shareholding in my
own welfare, I entrust it entirely to God and have confidence that God is
indeed working His purposes out (Phil. 2:13). Tough love indeed yet, as
in Israel's experience in Egypt, God's promises are resisted in ways that
lie beyond our understanding. When the complexities of life burden us
and the ways of God confuse, we are humbly to look to Jesus, 'gentle and
humble in heart', and find rest for our troubled heart (Matt. 11:29).

SCRIPTURE TO CONSIDER: Ps. 77:1–15; Dan. 10:2–19; John 5:16–30; Rom. 8:18–30.

AN ACTION TO TAKE: There are times when all we can do is to trust God in the
darkness that surrounds us. Waiting is challenging and we can only wait by
God's grace (Ps. 27:14).

A PRAYER TO MAKE: 'Lord, in the loneliness of the silence I wait for You. Come,
Lord Jesus. Amen.'

Numbers 14:17–23
**'Now may the Lord's strength be displayed, just as you
have declared: "The LORD is slow to anger, abounding
in love and forgiving sin and rebellion. Yet he does
not leave the guilty unpunished"' (vv17–18a)**

Many struggle with an apparent contradiction between the
God of the OT contrasted with the NT. Marcion (cAD 85–160)
attempted to distinguish between the NT's 'benevolent' God
and the 'malevolent creator god' of the OT. His early canon was
rejected, and the ministry of Jesus accepted as the fulfilment of the
OT narrative. So we are left with the picture of a God who exercises
judgment and to whom the whole of creation is accountable. There
are consequences to sin, as well as the means for forgiveness in Christ
Jesus. The gospel was made available through Jesus, and so those
living in OT times, whilst glimpsing what was to come, were unable to
receive redemption in their time.

The purpose of God is worked out over time and Israel's deliverance
from Egypt is a picture of the promised redemption established
through Jesus. God is consistent in His message, and in our own day
that same plan is unfolding, most often out of sight. The character of
God is unchanging and dependable, forgiving the repentant sinner,
whilst bringing judgment to those who reject His love. We do not have
the capacity to determine who is forgiven and who is judged by God
(Deut. 32:34–35), yet we do exercise responsibility to discern how best
we can respond to God through our lives and as the Church. This is
revealed through Scripture (both the OT and the NT), the story of God's
unfolding revelation from creation to the end of time itself.

SCRIPTURE TO CONSIDER: Num. 27:12–23; Ps 82; Matt. 7:1–6; 2 Cor. 5:1–10.

AN ACTION TO TAKE: We may have questions about our Christian faith. Many
have been raised and considered throughout history. You may find some
good answers to yours have been found already.

A PRAYER TO MAKE: 'Lord, help me to think through the consequences of my
decisions before I take action. Amen.'

Presence of God

Deuteronomy 4:5–8

'What other nation is so great as to have their gods near them the way the LORD our God is near us whenever we pray to him?'(v7)

The OT presents God's Law given to Moses in the Ten Commandments (Exod. 20). This was never replaced by Jesus – 'Do not think that I have come to abolish the Law or the Prophets; I have not come to abolish them but to fulfil them' (Matt. 5:17) – a fulfilment accomplished by Jesus inhabiting the Law. He now invites us to become a living expression of God's life on earth. This is not by becoming moral barometers throughout society, although many mistakenly make personal morality the foundational measure of Christian compliance. Jesus welcomed the most immoral into His circle, people who wouldn't have sought Him out if they thought He was leading on moral rearmament. Jesus encouraged His followers to live the essence of God's Law in practice; a life of presence not preaching.

Words have become a debased currency in our world of empty political promises and the mis-selling of the advertiser's craft. Even when fake news is fact-checked, the majority of people interviewed assume there must be some element of truth within the proven lie. There's a lack of role models across society, and whoever gets elevated by a media hungry for a hero is soon shown to have feet of clay. As disciples we acknowledge failings, have nothing to prove and live by God's provision. All we have to offer is Jesus, with whom we abide and who can recover the most broken of lives. Learning to live in God's presence is our first step to inhabiting the Law.

SCRIPTURE TO CONSIDER: Ps 139:7–18; Isa. 50:4–11; Col. 3:12–17; 1 Thess. 4:1–12.

AN ACTION TO TAKE: Is your faith about keeping rules? The Christian life is God's invitation to you to enjoy His presence and to become a point of His presence and beacon of hope in the world.

A PRAYER TO MAKE: 'Lord, help me to be a point of God's presence and a beacon of hope in the world every day. Amen.'

Write to micha@edwj.org and I'll write back personally and in confidence as soon as I can.

Deuteronomy 10:17–20
'For the LORD your God is God of gods and Lord of lords, the great God, mighty and awesome, who shows no partiality and accepts no bribes. He defends the cause of the fatherless and the widow, and loves the foreigner residing among you, giving them food and clothing.' (vv17–18)

I n an age of growing disillusionment with leadership, it is encouraging to note that God 'shows no partiality and accepts no bribes'. Strange that deceit has such a powerful pull on our human nature. I confess to having been tempted to cheat in my past, and historically there have been times when I have done so. I am not proud, but it took some years of walking with Jesus to discover that He wanted me voluntarily to let go of everything apart from my desire for Him. Today, even as I work at Waverley Abbey Trust (WAT), I am reassured that my responsibilities and position mean nothing to me and I am more than ready to return to my calling as a praying anchorite. Be encouraged; we can and will mature in our faith as we apply Scripture to all of life. God also offers a warm welcome to all. In our times of political correctness and 'cancel culture' we can have confidence that God embraces everyone. There are, of course, the gospel conditions for friendship with God, and He has embedded these into the heart of creation. Consequently, we shall have no success in attempting to reframe the gospel message. Inhabiting God's Law requires that we, like Jesus, are approachable by, and offer hospitality to, all. We cannot change the basis upon which eternal friendship with God is offered, but can communicate it through our actions as easily as our words. Love is most often felt before it is 'telt'.

SCRIPTURE TO CONSIDER: Lev. 19:32–37; Isa. 57:14–21; Luke 10:38–42; Heb. 13:1–10.

AN ACTION TO TAKE: How effectively are you able to offer hospitality to all? Are there unresolved inner conflicts to pray and work through?

A PRAYER TO MAKE: 'Lord, may I consistently learn to welcome everyone just as You daily welcome me. Amen.'

1 Samuel 17:45–47

**'This day the LORD will deliver you into my hands, and I'll strike you
down and cut off your head. This very day I will give the carcasses
of the Philistine army to the birds and the wild animals, and the
whole world will know that there is a God in Israel.' (v46)**

Whilst Christianity is often seen to be overwhelmed by current-thought leadership and offering little by way of creative responses to the cultural and social movements impacting global debate, we turn to the story of David who brought down an intimidating, warrior giant with a Stone-Age slingshot. It reminds us that what appears outdated, in the right hands can prove irresistible. Our biblical message has not run out of steam; we need to take hold of it and apply it in ways that address the primary questions dominating public discourse. Too often we shudder before the taunts of those seeking to dethrone God, and we find comfort in retreating to our campsite some distance from the frontline of the battle.

Engaging with the public discourse does not mean we need to change our dress; David was restricted when seeking the apparent protection of Saul's armour. He drew on the wisdom he had learnt as a shepherd, as we are to draw on all we have discovered of God. The debate will not be settled on rational grounds; here we will at best attain a score draw. God's wisdom lies beyond reason, although built of rational foundations. We must discover how to convey the nature of God's wisdom and create an opportunity for encounter between the human and the divine. The stone that gave David his success is an image of the resilience of divine truth in the face of impossible odds. We will never hold our ground by fighting swords with swords.

SCRIPTURE TO CONSIDER: 2 Chron. 32:6–8; 2 Sam. 22:31–37; 2 Cor. 3:1–11; 10:1–6.

AN ACTION TO TAKE: David approached Goliath with who he was and with what he knew. How does this influence your understanding of how you are to serve Jesus?

A PRAYER TO MAKE: 'Lord, I give You thanks that salvation belongs to You and that You are our deliverer. Amen.'

Psalm 33:10–15

'Blessed is the nation whose God is the LORD, the people he chose for his inheritance. From heaven the LORD looks down and sees all mankind' (vv12–13)

Our prayers are directed towards establishing God's rule so that all nations can enjoy God's blessing. It sounds simplistic, but Scripture declares that without God's authority chaos asserts itself. Whilst human brilliance is evident in the skill and speed of scientists creating a vaccine for Covid-19, such brilliance isn't the same as wisdom. Brilliance brings sudden flashes of insight; wisdom secures stability over an extended period of time through right judgment. Whilst humans may have beneficial moments of brilliance, we also see the fruit of such brilliance is exploited for great harm, such as nuclear fission. We celebrate brilliant advances in knowledge, but knowledge is no guarantor of wisdom.

Jesus is presented as 'wisdom from God' (1 Cor. 1:30), which means having the power of discerning and judging rightly. Here's how we all benefit, for God, who has created all things, enjoys unrivalled insight into how we might best order life from a personal to a national level. Whilst it's unfashionable to see Jesus as the source of wisdom, part of our learning is to find confidence that the Holy Spirit will lead us into all truth (John 16:13). Until we are convinced, we live a mixed message in the world, our place of witness. It's remarkable that we enjoy access to one who can truly lay claim to the title 'fount of all wisdom', yet our ability to access such wisdom, and consequently our confidence in advocating for God's rule, remains limited.

SCRIPTURE TO CONSIDER: Job 28:12–28; Ps. 14:1–4; Eph. 1:3–14; Heb. 4:12–16.

AN ACTION TO TAKE: Learning God's wisdom is essential in helping us live the Christian life. Consider buying a short study on Proverbs, God's book of wisdom, from edwj.org/mj22-18jun

A PRAYER TO MAKE: 'Lord, help me to discover more of Your wisdom and to place my full confidence in it as I pray for wise leadership worldwide. Amen.'

Isaiah 45:5–8

'I am the LORD, and there is no other; apart from me there is no God. I will strengthen you, though you have not acknowledged me, so that from the rising of the sun to the place of its setting people may know there is none besides me.' (vv5–6)

Isaiah prophesies about a blessed king who doesn't know Yahweh, the God of Israel, some 150 years before his rule. He speaks of Cyrus who reigned over the Babylonian empire from 539 to 530 BC. He gave the Jewish captives permission to return to Jerusalem. Without acknowledgement from Cyrus, God blesses him even though he never realised the significant role he was playing in God's plan. God's blessing is boundless and touches the lives of all those who live a godly life, regardless of their knowledge of God. The scale of God's blessing must always be borne in mind because we are far less generous than God. We want people to conform to models of understanding we've agreed and established, but God will not be constrained by our limited understanding. Jesus stood in an empty town square and, rather than fulfilling the letter of the Law, He told a woman caught in the act of adultery to 'go and sin no more' (John 8:11). God's heart seeks the salvation of all, not to prove a point at someone's expense. We have much we can learn both in the level of gratitude we are to express to God in our worship and in our willingness to open our total selves to collaborating expectantly with the Holy Spirit. It's good to learn to look for where we can encourage and bless rather than criticise and shame. Such encouragement creates a context within which God's life and love can flow most naturally.

SCRIPTURE TO CONSIDER: Ezra 4:1–4; Prov. 16:7–20; Luke 6:37–42; 1 Tim. 6:11–21.

AN ACTION TO TAKE: It might sound strange to learn that God blesses where and through whom He chooses. As a Christian, do you naturally seek to bless or to correct?

A PRAYER TO MAKE: 'Lord, enable me to look and see Your hand at work rather than impose my understanding on others, especially those with whom I disagree. Amen.'

Habakkuk 1:2–4
**'Why do you make me look at injustice? Why do you
tolerate wrongdoing? Destruction and violence are
before me; there is strife, and conflict abounds.' (v3)**

At 28 Camus wrote, 'Judging whether life is or is not worth living
amounts to answering the fundamental question of philosophy.'*
We all search for life's meaning to define our existence. Selwyn
Hughes argued that Significance (the opposite of meaningless) offered
one of three pillars offering a purposeful life, along with Security and
Self-Worth.** Our world reveals imbalances, peace and war, wealth
and poverty, and social development and environmental degradation.
Viktor Frankl, suffering in a concentration camp, considered what
motivated him to live. His conclusions were sharing his food, providing
emotional comfort to prisoners, and focusing on his love for wife
and family, also imprisoned. He wrote that for survival we need a
meaning for our life that gives hope and builds resilience.*** Habakkuk
considers his conflicted world, struggling with how to reconcile this
with God, who invites him to keep watching as he struggles with his
questions. We too are invited to talk with God and bring our questions
of meaning with all their many foci. Finally, in what I assume is a state of
mental and emotional exhaustion, Habakkuk quietly entrusts his need
for understanding to God's purpose, 'Though the fig-tree does not bud
and there are no grapes on the vines ...yet I will rejoice in the Lord, I
will be joyful in God my Saviour (Hab. 3:17a—18). Without abandoning
his search, he accepts that God's work is beyond his understanding,
requiring only trust. Disciples need a resilient faith.

SCRIPTURE TO CONSIDER: Isa. 55:8—13; Hab. 3:1—19; Matt. 6:19—34; Phil. 4:10—20.

AN ACTION TO TAKE: Ask, "What is the meaning of my life now?" Note your answers.
Now ask "What do I want my life to mean?" Compare your answers. What
decisions does this present?

A PRAYER TO MAKE: 'Lord, teach me to walk with You every day. Amen' (Hab. 3:19)

* The Myth of Sisyphus. 1942 philosophical essay by Albert Camus.
** Christ Empowered Living edwj.org/mj22-20jun   *** Man's Search For Meaning, Viktor Frankl (1946),

Isaiah 6:1–13

'Then I heard the voice of the Lord saying, "Whom shall I send? And who will go for us?" And I said, "Here am I. Send me!"' (v8)

A call is a summons or an invitation; its object determines which it is. God never overrides free will (Gen 3). We're often anxious about missing God's call, but this is unlikely. A call is always dependent on someone listening and responding. We're familiar with the phrase, 'There's none so deaf as those who do not wish to hear', an idiom taken from Scripture (Jer. 5:21–31). We are often anxious, both not to miss a call, but also about the object of that call; will it appeal to us or not?

A call is not something that needs to determine the shape of our whole life. Indeed, we may be summoned by God in different ways and at different times during our life. Having served in Youth for Christ and the Evangelical Alliance (UK) for the first part of my adult life, I was then called to learn (with much reluctance, frustration and clumsiness) to be the primary carer for my first wife. After she died, I applied for 64 jobs unsuccessfully before I heard the faint but persistent request that I pursue an anchorite's life of prayer, largely to withdraw from society and lead a prayer-oriented, ascetic life. This I did for 12 years until asked to serve WAT. I have retained my prayer rhythms, but life is far more active and engaging in this season. Learning to listen to God's call is a must for us all. A call is not defined by outcomes, nor does it require any recognition. All it requires, as Isaiah demonstrates, is obedience.

SCRIPTURE TO CONSIDER: 1 Sam. 3:1–10; Ps. 42:5–11; Eph. 1:11–23; 2 Tim. 1:3–14.

AN ACTION TO TAKE: Do you worry about missing God's call? Most often we can be scanning the horizon when God is inviting us to do something in our own backyard.

A PRAYER TO MAKE: 'Lord, I am ready to respond to Your call - may I be always listening for Your voice. Amen.'

Write to micha@edwj.org and I'll write back personally and in confidence as soon as I can.

Genesis 12:1–5

'So Abram went, as the LORD had told him; and Lot went with him. Abram was seventy-five years old when he set out from Harran.'(v4)

We often realise our call in the world through our obedience. We become a physical expression of God's call. Agnes Gonxha Bojaxhiu is best remembered for the work she led in the slums of Kolkata. However, initially principal of a Loreto Sisters school for girls, she was riding on a train from Kolkata to the Himalayan foothills for a retreat, when Christ called her to abandon teaching and work in the Kolkata slums serving the poorest and sickest. It took her 18 months to secure the approval of her Order, and with six months' basic medical training, ventured into Kolkata's slums with one goal, to serve those who are unwanted, unloved and uncared for. We know her as Mother Teresa and she epitomises unreserved care for society's marginalised and largely forgotten. She received a call when seeking God and it required energy and additional training to realise. It also established her as the embodiment of compassionate care for those who are excluded

Abram, meaning 'exalted father', gathers his family and sets out at God's invitation. As a consequence, he received a new name – Abraham, meaning 'exalted father of a multitude'. This was the realisation of God's promise. Yet, he also became the embodiment of faith itself (Gal. 3:6–9), and we are considered his children (multitude indeed) when we choose to live by faith rather than sight (2 Cor. 5:7). Others may well identify your call more clearly than you can. What is it you embody through your life?

SCRIPTURE TO CONSIDER: Judg. 6:11–18; 16:21–30; 1 Cor. 1:18–31; Heb. 11:8–19.

AN ACTION TO TAKE: What do you embody in life? Is this who you want to be and who God has created you to be? How can you make any changes you would like to?

A PRAYER TO MAKE: 'Lord, place me where I can best embody Your kingdom purpose with my life. Amen.'

The Gospel

Romans 1:14–17

'For I am not ashamed of the gospel, because it is the power of God that brings salvation to everyone who believes: first to the Jew, then to the Gentile. For in the gospel the righteousness of God is revealed – a righteousness that is by faith from first to last, just as it is written: "The righteous will live by faith."' (vv16–17)

What is the gospel? It is the unique and compelling announcement that God has restored the open relationship between Himself and His creation through the death and resurrection of Jesus. For me, this is indeed the heart of the good news that Jesus invited us all as disciples to make known to a world that is described as 'lost', which means wasted, ruined and worn out. God renews that same creation (Ps. 104:30) and through the gospel we are born again into a life that can be syncretised with the purpose of God, both for us and for the world we now seek to serve in Jesus' name (John 3:3). Salvation, the fruit of acceptance of the gospel, means preservation from destruction, danger and calamity. However, it's not salvation from life's troubles; rather the promise of eternal life following our death. Our mission is twofold: to accept the gospel with its promise of salvation for ourselves, and then to talk about it with others. Too often we seek to predict what questions someone else has, but it's best simply to speak in terms of why the gospel makes sense to us. Few are won by comprehensive theological expositions. Much more compelling is your story of why you have accepted Jesus as your Saviour and Lord. Our message is simple: Jesus dying but now risen and ascended. Whilst it might not seem much, it offers the key to unlocking the fullness of life for all who embrace its abiding message of hope.

SCRIPTURE TO CONSIDER: Ps. 102:25–28; Ezek. 34:20–31; Matt. 19:16–30; Heb. 10:11–14.

AN ACTION TO TAKE: The gospel is a life-giving message of hope. Do you have confidence in this simple gospel message?

A PRAYER TO MAKE: 'Lord, I am grateful to make my peace with You and look with confidence on my enduring friendship with Father, Son and Holy Spirit. Amen.'

1 Corinthians 15:1–17
'For what I received I passed on to you as of first importance: that Christ died for our sins according to the Scriptures, that he was buried, that he was raised on the third day according to the Scriptures' (vv3–4)

Jesus' death ended any need for a bloody sacrificial system and gave humanity the opportunity to taste and see God's goodness (Ps. 34:8). Once tasted, our hunger can never be assuaged by anything less than Jesus. He meets the human heart's deepest longing, something nothing else can satisfy. C. S. Lewis wrote:

'Creatures are not born with desires unless satisfaction for those desires exists. A baby feels hunger: well, there is such a thing as food. A duckling wants to swim: well, there is such a thing as water. People feel sexual desire: well, there is such a thing as sex. If I find in myself a desire which no experience in this world can satisfy, the most probable explanation is that I was made for another world.'*

We are a mass of competing desires that often lead us away from God's best. Many such desires are pursued in our honest search for fulfilment, love and acceptance, and to know self-worth. Too quickly what was once sweet upon the lips turns to bitter ashes, and our desire returns, unsatisfied. Unmet desire can lead to behaviours that are self-destructive, even when honestly pursued. Our gospel message is that God meets our every desire. My experience is that this takes a lifetime, and learning how to feed from Christ alone is a path born of sorrow, regret and pain. However, each stumble reawakens my desire for God and my resolve to pursue Him.

SCRIPTURE TO CONSIDER: Gen. 22:1–19; Ps. 37:1–7; Rom. 8:31–39; 1 Pet. 2:19–25.

AN ACTION TO TAKE: Are you disturbed by unmet desires? Acknowledge what they are, and the mistakes you have made seeking to meet them, and consider looking to God alone.

A PRAYER TO MAKE: 'Lord, thank You that You have chosen me. May I wait on You to meet my every desire. Amen.'

Write to micha@edwj.org and I'll write back personally and in confidence as soon as I can.

*C.S. Lewis, *Mere Christianity.* (1952) (London: Collins, 2016)

Sheep and Goats

Matthew 25:31–46

'When the Son of Man comes in his glory, and all the angels with him, he will sit on his glorious throne. All the nations will be gathered before him, and he will separate the people one from another as a shepherd separates the sheep from the goats.'(vv31–32)

In a time of obvious nervousness about what is acceptable, where carefully thought through perspectives are subject to 'cancel culture', it's perhaps essential we remind ourselves that we all ultimately go before a judge who will separate the wheat from the chaff, the good from the bad (Luke 3:17). In short, 'cancel culture' means preventing thought leaders from prominent public platforms or careers and polarising public opinion whilst stage-managing legitimate debate. Jesus engaged with all His critics, presented the gospel in robust terms, and clearly presented a day of judgment for the whole of humanity. Matthew describes this as the separation of the sheep and goats, which can be difficult to distinguish. I was once told that the distinction is in the ears; goats have sticky-out small ears, whilst sheep have flappers.

Regardless, the takeaway message is that there's a judgment coming, and whilst we can manage our own Christian PR so long as we still have breath, ultimately it's God's word that counts. The distinction here is that faith produces works that demonstrate God's loving heart. This is not to say that works can secure salvation. Peter described how that happens in his first sermon, 'Repent and be baptised, every one of you, in the name of Jesus Christ for the forgiveness of your sins. And you will receive the gift of the Holy Spirit' (Acts 2:38). However, faith gives birth to the evidence that reveals God's character and the mission produced through the Holy Spirit's work of sanctification.

SCRIPTURE TO CONSIDER: Ps. 78:52–55; Mal. 3:13–18; Matt. 13:18–30; 1 Cor. 4:4–21.

AN ACTION TO TAKE: Judgment means to focus our minds and help us take good decisions about what we really want out of life.

A PRAYER TO MAKE: 'Lord, may I live as one who sees the need and offers love in the name of Jesus. Amen.'

Equipped for Life

Corrie Ten Boom said, 'Every experience God gives us, every person he puts in our lives, is the perfect preparation for the future that only he can see'. Sent to Ravensbrück Concentration Camp by the Nazis for concealing Jewish families. Corrie emerged with a message of hope born from her experience of God's grace. Her unusual training equipped her to become as a significant witness to the power of forgiveness in a world constantly caught up in conflict. In EDWJ we will explore how God equips and empowers us to shape every event that impact with God, rather than being entirely bent out of shape.

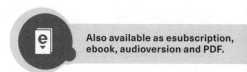

Also available as esubscription, ebook, audioversion and PDF.

Matthew 4:18–22

'Come, follow me,' Jesus said, 'and I will send you out to fish for people.' At once they left their nets and followed him.'(vv19–20)

J esus enjoyed a charisma that drew the crowds to Him to listen to His wise words. The Gospels contain those wise words, as remembered by those who followed Him. They were being collated within years of Jesus' death, so with plenty of eyewitnesses to contradict misinformation. We therefore accept that the NT gives an accurate picture of the life and thought of the earliest Christians. Jesus' invitation was a simple one, 'Come, follow me'. He had little difficulty in gathering a small and committed group of disciples. It was important to be with Jesus, yet His call encouraged individuals to consider how their trade might be used in the task of sharing their faith with those outside His immediate followers. This remains the challenge today. Whatever skills and experience we have, God will enable us to invest them in His service. And it's essential to recognise that service extends well beyond the walls of the church.

Often we can find it challenging to see where we might best be deployed. One reason we are developing practical courses at Waverley Abbey is to equip and mobilise disciples to learn how best to be the fisher folk Jesus calls and deploys. It's wonderful to think of a whole bank of confident, trained and equipped disciples distributed across communities throughout the UK. Waverley Abbey Ministries has been established to provide the training, to mobilise the Church and offer ongoing support to its members in active service.

SCRIPTURE TO CONSIDER: 1 Kgs 19:19–21; Ezek. 47:6–12; 2 Tim. 2:11–19; Gal. 1:11–24.

AN ACTION TO TAKE: Have you considered finding a suitable practical course to help train you for the ministry of serving Jesus in mission? Visit edwj.org/mj22-26jun

A PRAYER TO MAKE: 'Lord, help me to follow You and encourage others in finding faith and making their way in life. Amen.'

Luke 5:29–32
'Jesus answered them, "It is not the healthy who need a
doctor, but those who are ill. I have not come to call the
righteous, but sinners to repentance."' (vv31–32)

In the UK we enjoy free access to excellent medical support. Early diagnosis increases the chances of successful treatment. However, there is the risk that undiagnosed, underlying conditions remain untreated and could cause unexpected death. What's true of our physical health is true of our spiritual health. Jesus is our spiritual physician, but can only deal with what we bring for His diagnosis and treatment plan. Today, many voices seek to distinguish between the holy and the profane. Yet, we still lack the silver bullet to reduce spiralling social and mental health needs. In October 2020, The Centre for Mental Health estimated England's mental health services needed additional capacity for 10 million people (adults and children). Over the next five years, as a direct consequence of Covid-19, the estimated cost lies between £1.6bn and £3.6bn. Before the pandemic, mental health issues comprised 30% of GP caseloads. Neither human nor financial resources exist to respond to this challenge.* Jesus announces Himself the physician of human wellbeing. We are invited to join in His mission to support people to find fullness of life. Waverley Abbey trained ministers are available to offer chaplaincy support to GP surgeries. The Insight series and the course Introduction to Christian Care and Counselling offer a professional basic training to equip pastoral teams to offer mental health support and signposting to their immediate community. We can join Jesus' wellbeing ministry with some practical and focused training, essential for the mission of the Church. Is God calling you?

SCRIPTURE TO CONSIDER: Hos. 6:1–3; Jer. 8:14–22; Mark 5:25–34; John 6:41–69.

AN ACTION TO TAKE: Join Jesus the physician in supporting your local community. Train as a church or as an individual with Waverley Abbey College. Visit edwj. org/mj22-27jun1

A PRAYER TO MAKE: 'Lord, in You is my hope and my peace. May I take time to consult You and live according to Your diagnosis and treatment plan. Amen.'

*If you are finding life challenging and would like some help then please visit edwj.org/mj22-27jun2

Psalm 96: 1–6

'Declare his glory among the nations, his marvellous deeds among all peoples. For great is the LORD and most worthy of praise; he is to be feared above all gods.' (vv3–4)

My TV news watching has dropped to virtually zero. It seems most reporting is in reality opinion based on the few facts available. My prayer for this world is not improved by these opinion pieces; I have sufficient opinions of my own, often born of cynicism, political bias or grumpiness. Keeping as clear a conscience as possible and praying for God's glory to be revealed is challenging enough. Yet, Scripture consistently encourages us to give thanks and praise in the face of some devastating global situations. This is because, regardless of the machinations of humanity, from exploiting markets to political opportunism, God remains immoveable and Lord of all.

Encouragingly, we are invited to discover a fresh song of praise every day. I have little difficulty with this. It's not the need for something as yet unspoken, since there is nothing new under the sun (Eccl. 1:9). I use the same Orthodox liturgy daily and yet different elements break out and stir my heart and awaken my spirit to praise God every time. Reading Scripture daily, whilst the content doesn't change, God's word for us does. We are invited to enjoy a fresh encounter, moment by moment. Hence my annual reading plan becomes the daily source for my nurture and nourishment by God's Spirit. Whilst news hounds interpret global events, we can confidently daily declare that everything remains in the hands of God.

SCRIPTURE TO CONSIDER: Ps. 18:1–6; Jer. 10:6–13; Jude 1:17–25; Rev. 15:1–4.

AN ACTION TO TAKE: Do you see God behind the headlines and pray with confidence for God's will to be established on earth?

A PRAYER TO MAKE: 'Lord, teach me to sing Your praise for You are ruler of all, and the world and everything in it is sustained by Your Word. Amen.'

Write to micha@edwj.org and I'll write back personally and in confidence as soon as I can.

Jeremiah 20: 9–13

'But if I say, "I will not mention his word or speak any more in his name," his word is in my heart like a fire, a fire shut up in my bones. I am weary of holding it in; indeed, I cannot.' (v9)

Once surrendered to God, our attempts at denying Him only lead to greater inner turmoil. We're God's temples and, whilst we may 'cold shoulder' Him, we can't ignore His presence. Many of our faith struggles are a consequence of our unwillingness or inability to choose obedience. Yet let's not allow shame to distract us, for shame is only ever a tool provoking greater self-absorption and draws our gaze away from God. Our failures and struggles offer God the raw material from which He shapes us. It's one reason why we are to confess our sins to one another, both for the relief that comes from bringing our actual bad and good experiences into the open and for the encouragement of those we worship alongside.

Christianity is not a faith of perfection. We of course journey towards God and want to purge the waywardness that slows our spiritual formation, but it brings great reassurance when others know that we all fail yet are still loved by God and are invited to repent and start again – hopefully wiser and with greater resolve and appreciation of how God works in us. Too often we allow sin to silence us, when in fact the fire of God still burns within, demanding to express itself. I may feel wretched, yet that is precisely what a sinner is. God increases as I decrease (John 3:30), and such humility can only be born from my persistent failures. God knows us in our calling and patiently works with us without complaint. What a God we have!

SCRIPTURE TO CONSIDER: Deut. 8:1–9; Mic. 7:14–20; Luke 17:1–10; 1 Peter 4:1–11.

AN ACTION TO TAKE: Be encouraged that your failures offer the raw material Jesus needs to shape you. Are you willing to acknowledge your failings and surrender to God's shaping?

A PRAYER TO MAKE: 'Lord, may I be honest with myself, You and others and so allow You to make of me the witness You created me to become. Amen.'

Acts 3: 1–10

'So the man gave them his attention, expecting to get something from them. Then Peter said, "Silver or gold I do not have, but what I do have I give you. In the name of Jesus Christ of Nazareth, walk."' (vv5–6)

An urban legend attributed to Francis of Assisi (and others) describes how, on entering the Pope's presence, before whom a large sum of money was spread out, he observed, 'You see, the Church no longer can say, "Silver and gold have I none."' 'True, holy father,' Francis responded, 'but neither can it any longer say to the lame, "Rise up and walk"'. The point is, we can quickly lose sight of the God-life when engaged in life's minutiae. The issue is neither money nor physical healing, rather it's the essential ingredient of discipleship – the focus of our human heart. Peter and John are devoted to God, their only master, and when confronted by a challenge, they respond with the good news and inform the beggar that wealth is not his issue, it's his perception of himself and his world.

Jesus' teaching was often accompanied by a sign, and this man recovered his mobility, the feebleness in his legs replaced with active muscle tone. He rose to walk both physically and spiritually and experienced true conversion, a change of mind, no longer seeing himself as he, and others, had day after day. No one could now ignore him for he had a testimony to the love of God, and a mission to make God known. This beggar illustrates that prayer and mission are the principle gifts we bring through our lives to the many struggling in our world. All we have is Jesus, but then again, despite its deliberate sophistication, all the world needs is Jesus.

SCRIPTURE TO CONSIDER: Ps. 16; Matt. 6:19–27; Mark 5; Luke 7:1–10.

AN ACTION TO TAKE: As we conclude our reflections on mission, how will you prioritise your life going forward? All change takes time, and all effective change will lead us to Jesus.

A PRAYER TO MAKE: 'Lord, help me to keep You as my focus every day and grow in the confidence that all I need is Jesus, and Jesus is the greatest gift I bring to the world. Amen.'

Wellbeing Books

Invest in your personal and spiritual growth with books to support your mental health and wellbeing.

God's Plan for Your Wellbeing

Bouncing Forwards

Your Personal Encourager

Christ Empowered Living

Every Day Insights

The *Every Day Insights* series seeks to help those on a journey of learning, supporting others or facing difficult situations or emotions themselves to be supported each day.

Visit the link below for more information
wvly.org/mhw

Notes

Order form

Get Your **FREE** Daily Bible Reading Notes **TODAY! (UK ONLY)**

Your favourite Bible Reading notes are now available to you for FREE. God has called us back to the original vision of CWR to provide these notes to everyone who needs them, regardless of their circumstance or ability to pay. It is our desire to see these daily Bible reading notes used more widely, to see Christians grow in their relationship with Jesus on a daily basis and to see Him reflected in their everyday living. Clearly there are costs to provide this ministry and we are trusting in God's provision.

Could you be part of this vision? Do you have the desire to see lives transformed through a relationship with Jesus? **A small donation from you of just £2 a month, by direct debit, will make such a difference** Giving hope to someone in desperate need whilst you too grow deeper in your own relationship with Jesus.

4 Easy Ways To Order

1. Visit our online store at **waverleyabbeyresources.org/store**
2. Send this form together with your payment to:
   CWR, Waverley Abbey House, Waverley Lane, Farnham, Surrey GU9 8EP
3. Phone in your credit card order: **01252 784700** (Mon–Fri, 9.30am – 4.30pm)
4. Visit a Christian bookshop

For a list of our National Distributors, who supply countries outside the UK, visit waverleyabbeyresources.org/distributors

Your Details (required for orders and donations)

Full Name: CWR ID No. (if known):

Home Address:

         Postcode:

Telephone No. (for queries):   Email:

Publications

TITLE	QTY	PRICE	TOTAL
		Total Publications	

UK P&P: up to £24.99 = **£2.99**; £25.00 and over = **FREE**

Elsewhere P&P: up to £10 = **£4.95**; £10.01 – £50 = **£6.95**; £50.01 – £99.99 = **£10**; £100 and over = **£30**

Total Publications and P&P (please allow 14 days for delivery)   **A**

Payment Details

☐ I enclose a cheque made payable to CWR for the amount of: **£** _____

☐ Please charge my credit/debit card.

Cardholder's Name (in BLOCK CAPITALS) _____

Card No. ☐☐☐☐ ☐☐☐☐ ☐☐☐☐ ☐☐☐☐ ☐☐☐☐

Expires End ☐☐ ☐☐   Security Code ☐☐☐

Continued overleaf >>

One off Special Gift to CWR ☐ Please send me an acknowledgement of my gift **B** [   ]

GRAND TOTAL (Total of A & B) [   ]

Gift Aid (your home address required, see overleaf)

giftaid it I am a UK taxpayer and want CWR to reclaim the tax on all my donations for the four years prior to this year **and on** all donations I make from the date of this Gift Aid declaration until further notice.*

Taxpayer's Full Name (in BLOCK CAPITALS) _____

Signature _____ **Date** _____

*I am a UK taxpayer and understand that if I pay less Income Tax and/or Capital Gains Tax than the amount of Gift Aid claimed on all my donations in that tax year it is my responsibility to pay any difference.

Your FREE Daily Bible Reading Notes Order

	Please Tick	FREE	£2 pcm	£5 pcm	£10 pcm	Other
Every Day with Jesus (1yr, 6 issues)		☐	☐	☐	☐	☐ £_____
Large Print *Every Day with Jesus* (1yr, 6 issues)		☐	☐	☐	☐	☐ £_____
Inspiring Women Every Day (1yr, 6 issues)		☐	☐	☐	☐	☐ £_____

All CWR Bible reading notes are also available in single issue **ebook** and **email subscription** format. Visit **waverleyabbeyresources.org** for further info.

CWR Instruction to your Bank or Building Society to pay by Direct Debit
Please fill in the form and send to: CWR, Waverley Abbey House,
Waverley Lane, Farnham, Surrey GU9 8EP

DIRECT Debit

Name and full postal address of your Bank or Building Society

To: The Manager   Bank/Building Society

Address

_____

Postcode

Originator's Identification Number

4	2	0	4	8	7

Reference

Instruction to your Bank or Building Society

Please pay CWR Direct Debits from the account detailed in this Instruction subject to the safeguards assured by the Direct Debit Guarantee. I understand that this Instruction may remain with CWR and, if so, details will be passed electronically to my Bank/Building Society.

Name(s) of Account Holder(s)

Branch Sort Code

Bank/Building Society Account Number

Signature(s)

Date

Banks and Building Societies may not accept Direct Debit Instructions for some types of account

---

For a subscription outside of the UK please visit www.waverleyabbeyresources.org where you will find a list of our national distributors.

How would you like to hear from us? We would love to keep you up to date on all aspects of the CWR ministry, including; new publications, events & courses as well as how you can support us.

If you **DO** want to hear from us on email, please tick here [ ] If you **DO NOT** want us to contact you by post, please tick here [ ]
You can update your preferences at any time by contacting our customer services team on 01252 784 700. You can view our privacy policy online at waverleyabbeyresources.org